KU-010-421

THE US SPECIAL FORCES

WHAT EVERYONE NEEDS TO KNOW®

Also by John Prados

Operation Vulture: America's Dien Bien Phu

The Family Jewels: The CIA, Secrecy, and Presidential Power

Islands of Destiny: The Solomons Campaign and the Eclipse of the Rising Sun

In Country: Remembering the Vietnam War (written and edited)

Normandy Crucible: The Decisive Battle That Shaped World War II in Europe

How the Cold War Ended: Debating and Doing History

William Colby and the CIA: The Secret Wars of a Controversial Spymaster

Vietnam: The History of an Unwinnable War, 1945–1975

Safe for Democracy: The Secret Wars of the CIA

Hoodwinked: The Documents That Reveal How Bush Sold Us a War

Inside the Pentagon Papers (written and edited with Margaret Pratt Porter)

The White House Tapes: Eavesdropping on the President (written and edited)

Lost Crusader: The Secret Wars of CIA Director William Colby

America Confronts Terrorism (written and edited)

The Blood Road: The Ho Chi Minh Trail and the Vietnam War

President's Secret Wars: CIA and Pentagon Covert Operations from World War II through the Persian Gulf

Combined Fleet Decoded: The Secret History of U.S. Intelligence and the Japanese Navy in World War II

The Hidden History of the Vietnam War

Valley of Decision: The Siege of Khe Sanh (with Ray W. Stubbe)

Keepers of the Keys: A History of the National Security Council from Truman to Bush

Pentagon Games

The Soviet Estimate: U.S. Intelligence and Soviet Strategic Forces

The Sky Would Fall: The Secret U.S. Bombing Mission to Vietnam, 1954

THE US SPECIAL FORCES

WHAT EVERYONE NEEDS TO KNOW®

JOHN PRADOS

OXFORD
UNIVERSITY PRESS

Oxford University Press is a department of the University of
Oxford. It furthers the University's objective of excellence in research,
scholarship, and education by publishing worldwide.

Oxford   New York
Auckland   Cape Town   Dar es Salaam   Hong Kong   Karachi
Kuala Lumpur   Madrid   Melbourne   Mexico City   Nairobi
New Delhi   Shanghai   Taipei   Toronto

With offices in
Argentina   Austria   Brazil   Chile   Czech Republic   France   Greece
Guatemala   Hungary   Italy   Japan   Poland   Portugal   Singapore
South Korea   Switzerland   Thailand   Turkey   Ukraine   Vietnam

Oxford is a registered trademark of Oxford University Press
in the UK and certain other countries.

"What Everyone Needs to Know" is a registered trademark of
Oxford University Press.

Published in the United States of America by
Oxford University Press
198 Madison Avenue, New York, NY 10016

© John Prados 2015

All rights reserved. No part of this publication may be reproduced, stored
in a retrieval system, or transmitted, in any form or by any means, without
the prior permission in writing of Oxford University Press, or as expressly
permitted by law, by license, or under terms agreed with the appropriate
reproduction rights organization. Inquiries concerning reproduction
outside the scope of the above should be sent to the Rights
Department, Oxford University Press, at the address above.

You must not circulate this work in any other form
and you must impose this same condition on any acquirer.

Cataloging-in-Publication data is on file at the Library of Congress
ISBN 978–0–19–935428–3 (hbk.); 978–0–19–935429–0 (pbk.)

1 3 5 7 9 8 6 4 2
Printed in the United States of America
on acid-free paper

To all those who have given lives and careers
to America's Special Forces

Bearing the sword, and often the torch, messengers of the night within the land, bearers of a spark from the sacred fire. What greatness had not floated on the ebb of that river ... the dreams of men, the seed of commonwealths, the germs of empires.

—Joseph Conrad, *Heart of Darkness*

CONTENTS

INTRODUCTION

While President Barack Obama is taking measures to withdraw US forces from Afghanistan, moving to end the war there, there is every reason to suppose that US military efforts to fight terrorists will continue into the foreseeable future. In Afghanistan, against terrorism—indeed in all the fierce combats since the attacks of September 11, 2001—Special Operations Forces have taken center stage in American military actions. Under names like the US Special Operations Command, the Joint Special Operations Command, Special Operations Commands for the Army, Air Force, and Marines, the Naval Special Warfare Command, and a plethora of task forces, joint task forces, special weapons groups, psychological warfare battalions, civil affairs units, and much more, the shadow warriors of the Special Operations Forces (SOF) have been the tip of the spear. On any given day there are an average of 12,000 soldiers of the SOF on active operations in more than seventy countries. Yet the activities have been kept so quiet that the public perceives a nation at peace (save for the seemingly interminable conflict in Afghanistan and the recurrent one in Iraq and Syria).

A certain romanticism has attached itself to Special Forces. But despite their importance, the public's understanding of the genus remains very incomplete. Perhaps this is due to the romanticism itself, combined with the secrecy that the forces cultivate. Each new achievement—the raid that killed Osama bin Laden, the capture of Saddam Hussein, the demise of the drug lord Pablo Escobar—is celebrated. A unit here or there is remarked, whether SEAL Team Six or the Delta Force. Other times failures are mourned—the disastrous battle in a city in East Africa best known by the title of a book and movie, the failure of a lightning strike to rescue American hostages in Iran. These episodes, individually heroic or tragic, or both, have conditioned us to expect new exploits—but without affording us a basic knowledge of Special Operations Forces, their history, or who they are.

Meanwhile there are sources on the structure of this military elite at a given point in time—today, during John F. Kennedy's presidency, in World War II, and so on. Most works of that sort are like a snapshot, freezing SOF like a deer caught in the headlights. By and large these accounts focus on one or a few dramatic episodes—the exploits—while bypassing everything else. The truth, as will become evident, is that Special Operations Forces have undergone repeated transformations during the six decades in which they have had a formal existence within the American military. More than that, the developments that have made SOF the juggernaut they are today are not their brave ventures, but occurred during peacetime.

Two things are missing—a work that profiles Special Operations Forces as an evolving entity, from storied special mission force in World War II, to ostracized band of brothers in the US military of the 1950s, to recognized elite in Vietnam, back to the fringes in the 1970s—and then the steady rise to what we see today. That combines with an account that brings together within two covers the many SOF exploits plus the characters who populate this story. Capsule biographies explore some of those characters and their accomplishments. The other element is to frame this material in a simple, explanatory way rather than as a narrative account. This is the approach of this book. Its goal is both to furnish a brief overview of Special Operations Forces' history and to illuminate some boundaries of what can be expected from SOF as we move into the future.

ABBREVIATIONS

AFSOC	Air Force Special Operations Command
ARVN	Army of the Republic of Vietnam
BUD/s	Basic Underwater Demolition/SEAL
CBI	China-Burma-India (World War II combat theater)
CCC	Command Control Central (of SOG)
CCN	Command Control North (of SOG)
CCS	Command Control South (of SOG)
CENTCOM	Central Command
CIA	Central Intelligence Agency
CIDG	Civilian Irregular Defense Group
C-in-C	commander in chief
CO	commanding officer
FBI	Federal Bureau of Investigation
FOB	forward operating base
FOG	Field Operations Group
IED	improvised explosive device
ISA	intelligence support activity
JACK	Joint Army-CIA Korea
JCS	Joint Chiefs of Staff
JPRC	Joint Personnel Recovery Center
JSOC	Joint Special Operations Command
JSOTF	Joint Special Operations Task Force
LRP	Long-Range Penetration Patrol

MACSOG   Military Assistance Command (Vietnam)
            Studies and Observation Group
MACV   Military Assistance Command Vietnam
MACVSOG   Military Assistance Command Vietnam Studies
            and Observation Group
MARSOC   Marine Special Operations Command
MEB   Marine Expeditionary Brigade
MIT   Massachusetts Institute of Technology
NASA   National Aeronautics and Space
            Administration
NATO   North Atlantic Treaty Organization
NCO   noncommissioned officer
NLF   National Liberation Front
NROTC   Navy Reserve Officer Training Corps
NSA   National Security Agency
NSWC   Naval Special Warfare Command
NSWG   Naval Special Warfare Group
OCS   Officer Candidate School
ODA   Operational Detachment Alpha (A-Team)
OPLAN   Operations Plan
OSS   Office of Strategic Services
POW   prisoner of war
PRU   Provincial Reconnaissance Unit
ROTC   Reserve Officer Training Corps
RT   Reconnaissance Team
SAS   Special Air Service (British SOF)
SEAL   Sea, Air, Land soldier
SERE   Survival, Escape, Resistance, and Evasion
            (training program)
SF   Special Forces
SFG   Special Forces Group
SFOD   Special Forces Operational Detachment
SMO   Support to Military Operations
SOCOM   Special Operations Command
SOE   Special Operations Executive (British covert
            action agency)

SOF	Special Operations Forces
SOTF	Special Operations Task Force
STOL	short takeoff and landing (aircraft)
STS	Special Tactics Squadron (air force pathfinder SOF)
TWA	Trans-World Airlines
UAV	unmanned aerial vehicle
UCLA	University of California, Los Angeles
UCW	unconventional warfare
UDT	Underwater Demolition Team
USSF	US Special Forces
USSOCOM	US Special Operations Command
UW	unconventional warfare

PROLOGUE

BOOKENDS TO A WAR

ABSTRACT

The Afghan war dramatically illustrates the range of special operations roles and missions, showing in the Battle of Tora Bora, and in the raid that killed Osama bin Laden the spectrum of activities these troops carry out, as well as illustrating continuing themes that are common to this type of military activity.

The Afghanistan war began with high hopes and in a thrilling way. A few Americans—just a few—enlisted local allies and toppled the national government led by the Taliban, an Islamist political-religious movement that had emerged triumphant from a civil war and, in power, had shielded the extremist al-Qaeda, responsible for the September 11, 2001, terrorist attacks on the United States. The US response began just two weeks later. This campaign proved a signal victory for America's Special Operations Forces, marred only by the escape of al-Qaeda's leader, Osama bin Laden. Fast-forward almost precisely a decade—to May 2, 2011—and Special Operations Forces were the troops who would confront bin Laden again and kill him in a commando-style raid. In a broad sense these two episodes can be viewed as bookends for the American war in Afghanistan.

These two events—one the use of Special Operations Forces (SOF) to organize and support indigenous troops, the other a carefully prepared strike mission—also illustrate some of the classic SOF roles. They demonstrate the broad spectrum of uses to which these elite troops can be put. These scenes suggest both strengths and weaknesses of the Special Forces. Before investigating further it is worth setting this stage.

America's response to September 11—to go after al-Qaeda in its base area of Afghanistan—took place with power and speed. The first echelon, a Central Intelligence Agency (CIA) team, left the United States just over a week after the attacks. The team entered Afghanistan on September 26. Carrying a large amount of cash, the CIA team met with and enlisted the Northern Alliance, an Afghan tribal group that had been outraged when its leader was assassinated—in tandem with the 9/11 attacks—and that itched to go after the Taliban rulers, Osama bin Laden, and his jihadis. The entire venture was crafted on the fly. The CIA made first contact, but its initial team and another that followed simply did not have sufficient capacity for a country-wide military campaign. They also lacked the technical knowledge and expertise to serve as ground observers for US air attacks, which Washington used for its major firepower in this operation.

Those capabilities resided in the US Special Operations Command (USSOCOM)—Special Forces. The Special Forces had not only the wherewithal but the long-standing doctrinal role of carrying out precisely these kinds of missions. In US practice SOCOM is one of a constellation of what are called "unified commands," entities that incorporate elements of all the armed services to carry out their orders. Most of these, each led by a commander in chief, have a regional orientation. For example, the Central Command (CENTCOM), led by General Tommy Franks, held sway over Afghanistan and Iraq, among other places. SOCOM is a functional command, responsible for the care, feeding, and combat readiness of all US Special Forces. When a regional command like CENTCOM has an unconventional warfare mission or another need that falls within the Special Forces arena, SOCOM lends the appropriate units and experts to carry out the mission. Each of the regional commands has a subordinate "special operations command" controlled by its unified commander but administratively responsible to SOCOM. So it would be in Afghanistan. At CENTCOM navy vice admiral Bert Calland served as the regional chief for special operations.

General Franks had a contingency plan for war in Afghanistan, as all the unified commands have for the countries they watch, but CENTCOM's concept did not meet Washington's needs. The Franks plan amounted to an agglomeration of target lists for cruise missiles and, perhaps, aircraft. President George W. Bush demanded instant action after 9/11, on the ground; and Donald Rumsfeld, his secretary of defense, had been pushing for flexible and agile operations. The idea of a war in which the United States would contribute the major strike capability, in the form of American airpower, in alliance with an Afghan group on the ground, was closer to Rumsfeld's vision. It also represented a classic unconventional warfare initiative. The CENTCOM contingency plan made no provision at all for this kind of action. The Franks plan envisioned using Special Forces only for rescue missions.

Considering his options, General Franks threw the contingency plan out the window and recast the entire concept. Special operations would be critical. Indeed, Bert Calland's Special Operations Command Central, the SOF component of CENTCOM, would come to number more than three thousand operators in the Afghan theater. CENTCOM presented its plan in Washington on September 20, just as the lead CIA people left for the battle zone. The rapidity with which CENTCOM and SOCOM fashioned this venture is a fine illustration of the flexibility of these elite troops.

On October 5 a joint special operations task force took the field in Uzbekistan for rescues, and bombing began two days later. The headquarters supervised Colonel John Mulholland's

Fifth Special Forces Group, which took the field as Task Force Dagger. Mulholland's lead unit reached Afghanistan on October 19.

Dagger's troops were classic army Green Berets. For decades Special Forces operating units had been called "A-teams," but the nomenclature changed to Operational Detachments Alpha (ODAs) during the 1990s. These were groups of a dozen soldiers—noncommissioned officers led by a couple of officers—and each possessed a specific expertise while cross-training in other specialties. That way an ODA could train and advise local fighters across the full range of military tactics and functions. Air force forward air controllers with laser pointer equipment were added to the ODAs to coordinate the US close air support. Captain Mitch Nelson's ODA-595 became the first A-team to enter Afghanistan.

Nelson's team worked with the troops of General Abdul Rashid Dostum in the Mazar-e Sharif area of northern Afghanistan. Team 595 split into two groups to help Dostum. One rode with his cavalry and called themselves "The Horse Soldiers." Deploying just behind them, ODA-555 went to the Panjshir Valley and linked up with both CIA operatives and the main Northern Alliance forces under General Fahim Khan.

Special operations activity accelerated very quickly. The SOCOM had its own force of expert helicopter crewmen, the 160th Special Operations Aviation Regiment, nicknamed the "Night Stalkers," which proved critical in the thin air of Afghanistan, where valleys and even mountain passes were typically at eight or nine thousand feet above sea level. Many destinations lay at eleven thousand, and landing zones in the mountains, including the towering Hindu Kush, could be at thirteen or fourteen thousand feet height. In 2001 the army had little experience with high-altitude helicopter flying, so the Night Stalkers wrote the book for US chopper operations in the Afghan war.

Right with the choppers were the AC-130 gunships of the air force's First Special Operations Wing, which could orbit targets, dispensing immense amounts of ordnance from their automatic cannon and high-capacity machine guns. The gunships took center stage on October 19 when General Franks took the US campaign to the next level with the first ground strikes of the war. That night, preceded by a CIA Predator surveillance drone, the gunships hosed down targets for CENTCOM. Franks committed most of A Company, Third Battalion of the Army's Seventy-Fifth Ranger Regiment plus a reinforced squadron of the Delta Force to seize a desert landing strip southwest of Kandahar—Objective Rhino—and from there to raid the Taliban headquarters compound in Kandahar itself. The Rangers secured the airstrip, where an MC-130 "Combat Talon" transport landed within minutes, quickly followed by Night Stalker choppers to lift Delta operators to the Taliban objective. Meanwhile the rest of the Rangers plus some air force Special Tactics Squadron (STS) troopers captured a different desert airstrip to the west to become the first American base in-country. A few weeks later an American detachment, Marine Expeditionary Unit 15, returned to Rhino and established a more permanent presence.

At the end of October Admiral Calland, the Navy SEAL who sparkplugged special operations for General Franks, along with the CIA's task force chief, visited Afghanistan to assess the ongoing campaign. By late November the *only* regular US Army troops in-country were a reinforced company of the Tenth Mountain Division in eastern Afghanistan. Every other American was a SOCOM operator or a CIA officer or contractee. The special operations commitment included nine ODAs, parts of two Delta Force squadrons, Rangers, marines, Navy SEALs, and air force STS specialists, plus five or more CIA "Jawbreaker" teams. There were also more than a hundred British Special Forces and some Australian and French elite troops.

On November 9 Dostum's Eastern Alliance troops captured Mazar-e Sharif. A week later an armed Predator drone controlled by CIA eliminated al-Qaeda operations chief

Mohammed Atef. Cooperating with Afghan bands, small Special Forces had defeated the Taliban regime and were rapidly clearing the country. Kandahar fell on December 7. On the other side the Taliban and al-Qaeda forces had fragmented, remnants of each separately making their way toward Pakistan. Their retreat led to the Battle of Tora Bora, the most critical action of the invasion of Afghanistan and one conducted, on the American side, entirely by Special Forces and the CIA. Through a dozen days in December the fight against Osama bin Laden culminated in his escape into Pakistan.

Tora Bora turned out the way it did for many reasons, some of them illustrating the limitations of Special Operations Forces in their role as partisan warriors. The Americans did the best they could. Green Berets of ODA-572 plus CIA Jawbreaker Team Juliet were with the Afghan bands that moved toward Tora Bora, a pass through a wild mountain fastness at ten to twelve thousand feet that abutted the Pakistani border. They were joined by a detachment of Delta Force operators, Task Force 11 under the pseudonymous Major "Dalton Fury," who assumed command of all Americans in the area. But there were just ninety-one Americans involved, and they did not command the Afghan fighters.

The Pakistani XI Army Corps, supposed to block the other side of the border, formed a very porous seal. Gary Berntsen, the CIA's field commander in Afghanistan, begged headquarters for the insertion of a battalion of Rangers or marines on the Pakistani side who could create a hard block, but General Franks was not convinced, and President Bush and his senior advisers refused to override the CENTCOM commander. At a key moment al-Qaeda bribed one of the main bands of Afghan fighters to stay its hand, while others pulled back from the mountains at night in observance of Ramadan. The best Major Fury could do was to place observation posts through the area to call in massive amounts of aerial firepower. Fury maneuvered the outposts, and the US planes delivered tons of bombs, but the Americans could not order a serious ground attack, nor could they make one themselves. Special Forces tracked bin Laden's cell phone and brought successive air strikes on the locations they observed. But the al-Qaeda leader handed his cell phone to his chief of security and made for Pakistan while his lieutenant led the Americans off in a different direction. Osama bin Laden lived to fight another day.

From that day at Tora Bora the United States began a search for bin Laden that never let up. Bin Laden's escape left Special Forces operators with a score to settle. The CIA, National Security Agency (NSA), and other intelligence services were equally determined to succeed. Once, in July 2007, the generals and spies thought they had Osama in their sights. Again the locale would be Tora Bora, where a stream of intelligence suggested that al-Qaeda commanders and fighters were gathering. The spooks thought that bin Laden might appear there to lead a strategic review or christen some new attack plan. The generals laid on an action code-named Valiant Pursuit to get the enemy leader. Led by five B-2 Stealth bombers, an aerial armada would blast the Tora Bora area. Behind them would come US Special Forces, with artillery and gunship helicopters to back them up, to kill or capture anyone left by the aerial bombardment. Valiant Pursuit reportedly encompassed the largest special operation since the Vietnam War. But like Tommy Franks before him, CENTCOM's commander questioned the use of all those forces. Admiral William J. Fallon, the C-in-C, also found the intelligence more ambiguous than did his tactical commanders. Fallon called off Valiant Pursuit while the B-2 bombers were already in the air flying toward their targets.

But the quest did not return to square one. Different leads already under investigation would eventually permit the Americans to trace bin Laden to the house he occupied at Abbottabad, inside Pakistan. This sequence demonstrates the fundamental role intelligence plays in special operations. Cooperation between Pakistan and the United States after 9/11 included furnishing the cell phone numbers of suspected terrorists. From these the NSA identified one particular individual by his nom de guerre in 2002, and by tracking the phone and this Kuwaiti's movements over several years, the CIA and NSA were able to discover his real name and his role as an al-Qaeda courier. The courier was very careful, however, and the locations culled from his phone were mostly around Peshawar, many miles away from bin Laden. The Central Intelligence Agency continued to watch the Kuwaiti, and in the summer of 2010 one of its assets identified his white Suzuki vehicle in Peshawar. He was then followed to Abbottabad, more than two hours' drive away, where he went to a large house.

Agency operatives discovered the Kuwaiti owned the house. It seemed too big, even for the courier and his brother plus their families. Its cost had to have been much more than the courier could afford—US intelligence estimated the price to be equivalent to that of the entire 9/11 attack. The fact that the house had neither phone nor Internet connections, and that its occupants burned their trash, fueled more suspicion. The CIA had hoped that if it stayed behind the courier, he might lead them to bin Laden. Instead they began suspecting that bin Laden might actually be in that house. Agency director Leon Panetta briefed President Obama on the CIA's suspicions and sparked more intensive surveillance. By late 2010 US intelligence was confident that the Kuwaiti indeed worked for bin Laden.

The presence of the al-Qaeda chieftain himself proved impossible to establish. But a number of analysts were convinced of it, enough so that Panetta's confidence led President Obama to order up an action plan. At that point Vice Admiral William McRaven became involved. Chief of the Joint Special Operations Command, McRaven would craft the scheme for what became Operation Neptune Spear. Satellite photos showed the compound. The Central Intelligence Agency rented a house down the road from which to observe comings and goings. In the spring of 2011 it enlisted a Pakistani physician to use his project, administering free polio vaccines, in hopes of covertly securing family DNA samples from bin Laden relatives.

In the meantime Pentagon planners moved away from a concept like that of Valiant Pursuit—which had centered on big air strikes—and toward a lightning commando assault. A big bombing might go awry, and a drone attack—though involving less chance of collateral damage—would not guarantee neutralization. Neither would provide the desired assurance that bin Laden had actually been in the compound. Only direct observation could do that. Superiors told McRaven to get on the case. With a dozen or so of his top planners and senior commanders, the Red Bull–quaffing McRaven mapped out the operation. It would be a familiar kind of sally—a direct action—something Special Forces did many times every day in Iraq and Afghanistan. The problem here lay in mounting a raid 150 miles from US bases, one inside Pakistan, a restive ally already disquieted by US drone attacks and rent by fissures between its military and intelligence services on the one side, and its political leadership on the other. Some American officials were convinced that Pakistani intelligence actually aided al-Qaeda. However, Bill McRaven, who had fashioned a theory of special operations for his thesis at the Naval Postgraduate School, felt sure the thing could be done.

Admiral McRaven selected Navy Special Forces—"Sea, Air, Land Soldiers" universally known as SEALs—to carry out the raid. Within the SEALs McRaven chose its counterterrorism unit, Seal Team Six, an elite within an elite, which had the cover name Naval Special Warfare Development Group. Team Six had a Red Squadron of its best operators, but there were other good men too. The group chose its top SEALs and gave them the mission, starting with a practice deployment to North Carolina.

Whether to involve the Pakistanis and how much to tell them were key headaches solved above the level of the assault team. The dilemma worsened early in 2011 when a CIA contractor in Lahore killed two locals he claimed were trying to rob him. The incident led to an uproar in Pakistan, the exposure of the Central Intelligence Agency station chief there, and fresh Pakistani objections to American activities in that country. The net effect was to ensure there would be no joint mission, and only a last-minute notification to the Pakistanis that the United States was mounting an operation inside their country. Admiral McRaven planned on the basis that US troops might end up in a firefight with Pakistani soldiers, so he put together a larger quick reaction force, separate from the SEAL assault team, and prepared to intervene if necessary.

On March 14 the issues were debated before President Obama, who approved testing feasibility of the raid option. The SEAL team practiced on a replica of the bin Laden compound created for this purpose in North Carolina, and rehearsed the entire mission in the high plains of Nevada, where the altitude was closer to conditions at Abbottabad. Obama settled on the raid plan in April and thereafter held repeated meetings to review its progress. On April 19 he agreed that the mission force should move to Afghanistan, from where the raid would originate.

Timing was critical. McRaven would use another SOCOM unit, the army's Night Stalkers, to fly the SEALs to Abbottabad in helicopters. They wanted the advantage of darkness—the Americans would use low-light vision goggles—and the night of April 30 was the new moon. To complete the final preparations the SEALs began moving to Afghanistan on April 26, and the other men and equipment assembled at the launch base. President Obama, still with no certainty that bin Laden actually lived in the house in Abbottabad, gave the go-ahead after a White House meeting two days later. Obama appeared and traded jibes with reporters at the White House Correspondents' Dinner in the evening of April 30. Around that time, from his Joint Special Operations Command forward headquarters at Bagram airbase, Admiral McRaven put his forces in motion.

It was the afternoon of May 1 in Washington, but just after midnight in Abbottabad, when the SEAL raid took place. The assault group of twenty-three operators and a dog, plus an interpreter, flew in two stealth helicopters that kept very low to evade possible radar detection. A spare chopper, a larger Chinook, went along for any emergency. Another unit of twenty-four SEALs followed in several more Chinooks and stopped at an intermediate landing zone. They would provide the reaction force plus refuel the Night Stalkers' mission choppers. One of the stealth craft crashed on landing, losing its tail rotor, but the SEALs landed successfully. The spare ship had to be called in for the extraction. That turned out to be the sole imperfection in the raid.

The Team Six operators broke into their assault and support groups and made their way into the house. The Kuwaiti courier, his brother, and Osama bin Laden all perished in the attack. Some members of all three families were wounded. Operators sent the message "Geronimo," signifying to McRaven and President Obama that the enemy leader had been secured. Soon enough they learned bin Laden was dead. Neptune Spear had been a complete success.

These recent events have been recounted in this degree of detail because they illustrate a number of features of special operations. In the first place Tora Bora and Abbottabad represent two ends of the spectrum of Special Forces' activity. The Afghan invasion and Tora Bora show Special Forces in their role as instigators and facilitators for larger bands of indigenous troops. The invasion would never have succeeded without the alliances made with Afghans opposed to the Taliban. Special forces also exhibited their prowess as point men for other elements of military might, in this case the aircraft that inflicted much of the damage on the enemy. The failure at Tora Bora also suggests another facet of the special operations equation—the need for larger ground forces to supplement the elite troops for specific purposes. Skilled and heavily armed as they were, the ODAs just did not have enough bodies to block all of Osama bin Laden's potential escape routes.

Both Tora Bora and Neptune Spear reveal the large part that intelligence plays in effective special operations. Communications intercepts placed bin Laden in the mountain fastness, but there was never enough information to trap him, and the terrorists' own deceptive measures utilizing the same communications devices helped the adversary escape. Thereafter the importance of intelligence in tracing bin Laden to Abbottabad is quite evident. But the intelligence for Neptune Spear was also imperfect. President Obama, Admiral McRaven, and the others who collaborated on this mission never had complete assurance of the presence of their enemy. Moreover, the SEALs lacked complete information as to their target. The internal layout of bin Laden's house, the number of people actually there, their armament—all remained unknown until the moment of contact. The success at Abbottabad suggests that while intelligence is a vital factor in special operations, knowledge of the enemy is often imperfect, and yet this does not preclude success. The goal of Special Operations Forces is to be good enough, and strong enough, to win despite the shortcomings of intelligence.

Neptune Spear unfolded as an exemplar of the commando raid, a "direct action." This function of Special Operations Forces is at the opposite end of their spectrum. Vital missions of this sort often draw the personal attention of presidents. To a degree not matched in most military endeavors special operations involve the highest levels of government—secretaries of defense, the National Security Council, and the generals, all closely coordinating the actions of handfuls of skilled soldiers in the field. How it is that special operations acquired this vital importance is where we now turn.

1

ORIGIN OF THE SPECIES

ABSTRACT

History contains examples of special military operations stretching back to antiquity, but specific forces oriented to these kinds of missions are a more recent development. The earliest were Rangers. A pattern also emerged of nations creating special forces in times of conflict and then disbanding them in times of peace. The US experience followed this pattern as late as World War II, when Special Forces had broad roles and missions but were nevertheless sidelined in the aftermath. The need for these kinds of forces re-emerged in the Korean War and was given impetus by the Cold War confrontation with the Soviet Union, when Special Forces became a permanent feature of the US military.

Critical to the antecedents of modern Special Operations Forces is the question of how you define their mission. If the notion is that these troops are bands of heroes, then their history can be traced into antiquity, for in warfare there has always been a place for the handpicked soldier entrusted with a critical mission. If, on the other hand, the definition involves an elite body of troops constituted for irregular warfare, then their origin is more recent. The idea of soldiers picked, trained, and organized for *special* activities traces only to the Middle Ages. Over time the spectrum of missions for such troops expanded and became well accepted. But for a long time the forces were ad hoc groupings. No matter which way you trace the history, the events of World War II proved central to the evolution of the species, for between 1939 and 1945 military innovators developed standard techniques and patterns of organization. Specific units and their roles may vary over time and from one nation to another, but the sense that armies should have regular forces and capabilities oriented toward a spectrum of special missions continues into the present day.

What about the Trojan Horse?

The "band of heroes" narrative stretches back into history, fiction, even the Bible. Homer tells the story in *The Iliad* of the deception that amounted to what was basically a commando mission—the Trojan Horse, supposedly left for tribute outside the enemy fortress, but containing picked fighters inside whose purpose was to strike the adversary's most vulnerable point, opening the gates to the avenging swords of the main army. Cities in Palestine, castles in the Dark Ages, forests and mountains, the high seas, all became locales for what can be called special action. Warriors striking by stealth, whether brigands or troops, have played key roles at critical moments. One way to think about this is that the *missions* became established before the *capabilities.* A leader might want to surprise the enemy, as with the Trojan Horse itself; another could aim to harass the adversary as they moved through the land, or the goal might be to reach behind the opponent and strike where they were not prepared. These tactics can be pictured as *irregular warfare,* in today's idiom "unconventional warfare," or techniques.

For a long time these kinds of military actions developed by serendipity. They were situation-specific. A leader would see an important need, pick soldiers to execute the mission, and loose them on the enemy. A band of fighters, cut off, would inflict whatever mayhem they could. Resisters among an oppressed population could rise against their tormentors. Conversely, a village or lord might enlist a few good men to protect the land and warn of the approach of enemies. Scouting, ambush, and—again to use a modern idiom—"asymmetrical warfare" were the recognized stuff of special operations. Possibly the first fighters permanently engaged in these kinds of operations were called "rangers," and their mission was just that: to range the land as instructed by their liege.

History records that the king of England employed rangers to protect forests from brigands as early as the fourteenth century. These rangers were individuals or small bands. In the New World, the colony of Virginia hired a ranger to protect its Kent Island (now part of Maryland) in 1634. Plantation owners in Virginia and Maryland employed small parties of rangers to fight marauding Native Americans. Those two colonies coordinated a ranger mission in 1676, about the time the colonies of Plymouth and Massachusetts formed their own rangers. New York and Georgia recruited rangers for the War of Jenkins' Ear (1739–42) and King George's War (1739–48). But no doubt the best known of these early formations, formed in 1756 as the Ranger Company of the New Hampshire Provincial Regiment, was Rogers' Rangers. Major Robert Rogers not only created this unit, he issued standing orders that succinctly instructed his men on principles of irregular warfare. His principles can be considered the first special operations doctrine, and they are still taught today in training for these elite warriors. Rogers' Rangers had an important scouting and raiding role during the French and Indian War (1756–63), successful enough that French enemies countered with antiranger companies.

At the outset of the American Revolution, in 1775, the Continental Congress ordered the creation of ten companies of expert riflemen, but these rangers largely played local roles. More important were the Corps of Rangers that General George Washington formed under Colonel Daniel Morgan in 1777—who were effective against the British at the battles of Saratoga (1777) and Cowpens (1781)—and the partisans of Francis Marion, the "Swamp Fox," who were thorns in British sides in the Carolinas throughout the conflict. Other companies of rangers fought on both the Continental and British sides in the war.

But the pattern of picked men for specific missions persisted. When the ranger companies mustered out, the nascent US Army made no effort to preserve them. Similarly, rangers were recruited for the War of 1812 but disbanded afterward. And in the Civil War there were many irregular units on both sides—again without lasting impact on the US military. The American Civil War is replete with instances of reliance upon irregular troops. Most prominent on the Confederate side were the bands led by John Singleton Mosby, Turner Ashby, and John Hunt Morgan. On the Union side the First Regiment of Mounted Rangers was formed in Minnesota. Some of these rangers remained in service along the frontier after the war, the first instance of a regularized adaptation of the scouting and raiding mission, but in the 1880s their remaining elements were absorbed into the Texas Rangers, a state ranger force that had existed since that state's time as an independent republic. Between that time and World War II the US military made little use of Special Forces.

What Happened in World War II?

The conflict of 1939–45, which the United States entered in 1941, proved to be the moment of genesis for American Special Forces, starting with the creation of regular Ranger battalions but involving a wide array of unconventional capabilities. The demands of the war and the example of our British allies drove the enterprise. The events of the war defined the spectrum of missions that have been subsumed under the rubric of "unconventional warfare" ever since: raids or penetrations of a hostile coast; sabotage of enemy facilities; "long-range penetration," or missions deep into the opponent's rear inserted by land, sea, or air; covert scouting of key targets; underwater sabotage or reconnaissance; liaison with or training of indigenous resistance forces; plus key missions assigned by senior commanders that are thought to require expert, highly experienced forces.

The British faced many challenges, including the fact that they had been driven off the continent of Europe but still needed to exert a presence there, needed to support a European resistance against German occupiers, and required a capability to carry out special missions in such exotic environments as the deserts of North Africa, the jungles of Burma, and the fjords of Norway. To meet these demands our allies formed "Commandos," elite units of highly trained soldiers in both the British Army and Royal Marines; along with such exotic units as the Long Range Desert Group, the Gideon Force in East Africa, the "Chindits" of the British Indian Army, the Special Boat Section, Special Air Service, Special Operations Executive, and Z Force of the Australian Army. Most of these entities were created between 1940 and 1942, and when the United States entered the war, American leaders quickly appreciated their value and moved to replicate their capabilities.

First up on the American side were the Rangers. Their leading unit, Major William O. Darby's First Ranger Battalion, was drawn from volunteers from other conventional forces and created in Northern Ireland in the summer of 1942. "Darby's Rangers" demonstrated their effectiveness in the campaigns in Northwest Africa, Sicily, and Italy. Before the war had ended, seven US Ranger battalions were created. Most of Darby's unit and another were captured by the Germans during the beachhead battles for Anzio in Italy. A provisional Ranger unit, before it was disbanded, helped British commandos in several raids in Norway. The Second Ranger Battalion famously assaulted Pointe du Hoc, a German strongpoint near Omaha Beach, on D-Day in Normandy. The Fifth Rangers also participated in the Omaha battle. The Sixth Ranger Battalion, sent to the Pacific, played an important part in the Philippine landings in 1944–45 and notably liberated Filipino and American prisoners held in a camp at Cabanatuan in January 1945. Working with them were the Alamo Scouts, a volunteer reconnaissance unit performing the same functions created by the Sixth Army of General Douglas MacArthur's Southwest Pacific Theater of Operations.

Galahad Force, another Ranger unit (formally the 5307th Composite Unit [Provisional]), became the largest US combat force in the Burma theater. Called "Merrill's Marauders" after its leader, Brigadier General Frank D. Merrill, the Marauders made a daring outflanking march behind Japanese lines to become the anvil against which Nationalist Chinese troops would hammer the enemy. Galahad Force is recorded as having marched more than a thousand miles through the Burmese jungles in the spring of 1944.

Laboring alongside the Marauders, Detachment 101 from the Office of Strategic Services (OSS) organized, equipped, and led bands of tribesmen known as the Kachin Rangers, who harassed the Japanese and screened the operations of Galahad Force and of the British Chindits, parachuted into the same region. In Thailand during the last months of the war OSS operatives also had great success in mobilizing partisan fighters against the Japanese. The Office of Strategic Services, America's wartime spy agency and the forerunner of today's Central Intelligence Agency (CIA), created several kinds of Special Forces, of which Detachment 101 is only one example. Another would be the "Operational Group," trained and equipped for specific missions but along the lines of a British commando unit. Then there were the "Jedburgh" teams, named for a town in Scotland where the troopers trained, composed of OSS men grouped together with British operatives and fighters from France or other lands, and intended to work directly with Resistance partisans in Western Europe. Nearly a hundred OSS men were assigned to the Jeds, including future CIA director William Colby and several officers who would subsequently hold key Special Forces commands in the Vietnam War. Efforts of the Operational Groups peaked in early 1945, when there were seventy-five of these teams working in France alone.

The Philippines became the locale for what was probably the most significant Resistance-type movement in the Pacific. American and Filipino soldiers who had evaded capture when the Japanese overran the islands began to fight back, organizing into bands and gradually linking up with each other to coordinate their activities. Eventually they established communications with General Douglas MacArthur's command in Australia, arranging for supply shipments by submarine. MacArthur, who kept the OSS out of his theater, ended up with some 15,000 partisans in the Philippines, a force larger than the Kachin Rangers. Ironically, the Philippine partisans, who became one of the models for the eventual creation of American Special Forces, were a product of the only military command in World War II that rejected the help of the OSS Special Forces of the time.

The US Marine Corps, recognizing the need for highly trained units of troops for raiding and reconnaissance purposes, formed two Marine Raider Battalions. Although these would later be folded into other marine formations, the Raiders executed important combat missions in the Solomons and Gilbert Islands.

Those early combat landings convinced fleet commanders that better information on hostile shores was necessary. The US Navy moved to create its first Underwater Demolition Team (UDT). In the French North Africa amphibious landing of late 1942, ad hoc UDTs cleared obstacles that permitted the landing of Darby's Rangers. Underwater Demolition Teams were sent to the Mediterranean and to MacArthur. The navy organized Scouts and Raiders at Little Creek, Virginia, which remains a major SEAL base today. The army and navy together established an Amphibious Scout and Raider School at Fort Pierce, Florida.

Navy teams succeeded in clearing eight paths through the German obstacles on Omaha Beach during the D-Day landings. The largest UDT mission of the war took place during the 1945 invasion of Okinawa with teams totaling nearly a thousand combat swimmers. These "frogmen" totaled about 3,500 at the end of the war.

To support special missions, Jedburghs, the Resistance, and similar unconventional warfare missions, the Army Air Force assigned some of its bomber groups to full-time work with the soldiers and sailors. These became known as "Carpetbaggers." And in the China/Burma/India theater, "Air Commando" groups were formed that mixed transport and strike capabilities together to succor units like Galahad Force and Detachment 101 and give them air support.

Where Did Special Forces Go after the War?

As World War II ended, the future of unconventional warfare forces hung in the balance. What would emerge as the standard arguments against these techniques and forces already existed in embryo. Field officers of the other combat branches tended to look askance at these exotic units. One powerful claim was that conventional forces could perform the same tasks. In terms of raw numbers of enemy killed, that was probably true; but the assertion gave little credit to the elite units for the key missions they had carried out, and targets they had neutralized, at crucial moments during the campaigns. Regulars also disdained the glamorization of the exotic units, such as Merrill's Marauders, the subject of much favorable publicity. The idea that the unconventional forces consumed resources and siphoned off skilled soldiers that could benefit the military at large was already being articulated.

The question became whether the US military would repeat its pattern of dispensing with unconventional warfare once the immediate need seemed to have passed. As with the Marine Raiders, both the Carpetbaggers and Air Commandos were reassigned to more standard activities before the war even ended. President Harry S. Truman disbanded the OSS in September 1945. But the navy kept a pair of its UDTs even if they were at half strength. And the army, though it also disbanded the Ranger battalions and Marauders, kept in mind the mission of organizing resistance behind enemy lines, and experimented with "airborne reconnaissance units" between 1946 and 1948. The units were even to be called "Rangers." But their organizational model, with a high proportion of officers to enlisted soldiers (115 of the former, 135 of the latter) in a "company" or "group," seemed to aim at conducting partisan activities in support of a conventional battle. The groups would be attached to armies for both irregular warfare and commando-style missions.

None of these units were actually formed. Officials were still debating their merits when new elements entered the equation. The first key event was the emergence of the Cold War. That led to creation of the CIA, and alongside it a covert operations unit called the Office of Policy Coordination. This entity specifically sought to create resistance to the Soviet Union, both internally and in the territories Moscow controlled. Another factor was the civil war in Greece, where US military assistance to the anti-communist Greek government against a communist insurgency created a demand for the kinds of expertise the United States had nurtured in the OSS and its unconventional forces. As the CIA sought expert help, more and more officers who had come up through the ranks of the unconventional warriors found themselves assigned to duty on the front lines of the Cold War.

How about Special Forces in Korea?

The pendulum began to swing as military commanders and government officials recognized a need that could not be met by conventional forces. With the beginning of the Korean War in June 1950 the US military quickly rediscovered its need for all the sorts of unconventional forces it had relied upon in the big war. The military activated a Ranger company for the Eighth Army command two months into the conflict and then, in a frenzy of activity, sixteen more between that October and February 1951. These were direct action units, mostly assigned to infantry divisions. They were taken out of service in 1951, but Ranger training continued with the purpose of having a cadre of qualified experts in every army unit. About 700 Army Rangers, a couple of hundred marines in a provisional raider unit, a hundred UDT sailors, and nearly 250 British Royal Marine Commandos made up the United Nations special warfare force.

Almost simultaneously new entities appeared in Korea to focus on partisan activities akin to those of OSS Detachment 101 with the Kachin Rangers, or the British SOE with the Resistance in Europe. At least a half-dozen of these organizations materialized, or perhaps it would be more accurate to say that a special operations capability was created and then existed under a succession of cover names. It morphed constantly, mixing military and CIA officers in a kaleidoscope of patterns.

The nature of the war in Korea led to a particular style of operations. The Korean peninsula's relatively small expanse posed problems. North Korea's tight political controls limited the ability to recruit partisans. In particular after the late 1950 intervention by the People's Republic of China, enemy troop density was very high and impeded operations. The difficult terrain complicated supply problems for troops in action. On the other hand there were many offshore islands ringing the peninsula. Special Forces began making incursions onto the islands, establishing bases on them, and then mounting attacks on the mainland. Unconventional warfare more resembled the commando raids of World War II than it did the Resistance war.

By 1952 the island-based raiding force was known as the Far East Liaison Detachment (Korea). An army component, the 8240th Army Unit, ran the offshore partisans. Sections Leopard, Wolfpack, and Kirkland were the field commands. Typically an American leader, senior staff, and communications specialists squired forces of Korean partisans. For example, Section Wolfpack in March 1952 had seven Americans but planned to recruit 4,000 Korean fighters. Some months later there were a dozen Americans for 6,800 Koreans. At that time Leopard was reporting its strength at 5,500. A few months later the high command reorganized again, taking cadres from this force to create the United Nations Partisan Forces Korea, which it anticipated would attain a strength of up to 20,000 within a few months.

The air force also replicated its Carpetbaggers from the big war. This began with a detachment of the Twenty-First Troop Carrier Squadron. Captain Henry ("Heinie") Aderholt led this unit, which made supply drops and inserted agents throughout the theater. He used volunteers from his and other squadrons to fly low-altitude night missions, employed them for a month, and then sent them back to their units. On the offshore islands that lacked airfields, planes would land on the beach at low tide, doff their loads, then fly away before the water came up. Throughout the war the Carpetbaggers lost only two aircraft.

Air commanders also created an Air Resupply and Communications Service, with wings stationed in Europe, in the continental United States, and at Clark Air Force Base in the Philippines. The wings moved supplies, dropped leaflets, broadcast propaganda on loudspeakers, and flew liaison missions, using a mixture of B-29 bombers, flying boats, transport planes, and early model helicopters. The best-known—if not much celebrated—mission over Korea took place on January 15, 1953, when "Stardust 40," a 581st Wing B-29 piloted by wing commander Colonel John K. Arnold, was shot down near the Chinese border. Three men died. Arnold and seven other crewmen bailed out and were captured. Held as war criminals, they were put on trial in Beijing, accused of making germ warfare attacks on China. There has been a persistent controversy over the veracity of these claimed attacks. The US airmen were released in 1955. The air force had meanwhile deactivated the special warfare units.

What Happened in the Cold War?

Cold War competition put a premium on propaganda, which in the US military was the province of "psychological warfare," another unconventional technique that had been given a powerful impetus by World War II. President Truman had an abiding interest in these tactics. In 1951 Truman established the Psychological Strategy Board as the unit of his National Security Council apparatus responsible both for spurring propaganda plans of all types and for approving US covert operations. The conjunction of psychological and unconventional warfare would result in the revival of Special Forces.

In 1950 the army created a chief of psychological warfare at the headquarters level. Robert McClure, who would rise to be a major general, got the assignment. In World War II McClure had been the chief of psychological operations for the supreme allied commander, Dwight D. Eisenhower. McClure's staff division not only supervised "psy-war" efforts in Korea, it took on the special operations portfolio. General McClure gathered a small group of officers who had led partisan resistance in the Philippines, or had fought with Merrill's Marauders or with the OSS in Burma, China, Yugoslavia, and elsewhere. These men reviewed the record, convincing themselves that fomenting partisan resistance in war should be the goal for an unconventional warfare force, and that peacetime preparation would optimize that function. They encouraged General McClure to propose the creation of "Special Forces." The general, very receptive to the proposal, also had a good relationship with army chief of staff General J. Lawton Collins, who liked the idea and pushed it through army channels.

At Fayetteville, North Carolina, home to the army's huge airborne base Fort Bragg, General McClure had a Psychological Warfare Center. There, on June 20, 1952, the army created its Tenth Special Forces Group (Airborne), under Colonel Aaron Bank, a veteran of OSS missions from World War II and one of the unconventional warfare advocates from McClure's office. Colonel Bank began with just ten men in his group. They were relegated to an abandoned barracks at a back corner of Bragg known as "Smoke Bomb Hill." Since that day more than six decades ago, the United States has never been without Special Forces. Indeed they outlived the original infatuation with psy-war—the Psychological Warfare Center at Bragg would be supplanted by a (still extant) Special Warfare Center toward the end of 1956.

Very early on the Special Forces adopted the basic pattern of organization they have ever since maintained. The term "operational detachment" was quickly adopted but not used in the field. There were four echelons of command. The field unit was the "A-Team" (hence the current nomenclature "Operational Detachment A"). These teams were to recruit, train, and lead partisans or to perform special missions. At the intermediate level the B-Team would command all the bands in a region and furnish supplies and support to the field units. The C-Team was intended to perform the same functions for all Special Forces in a country, and the D-Team, a regional command, would control forces in two or more countries. The C-Team could be likened to an infantry company. The B- and C-Teams could be divided between a forward headquarters in the field and a rear echelon organizing the support and located at a "Special Forces Operating Base." With the aim of fomenting behind-the-lines resistance to an enemy—at that time Soviet—occupier, the Tenth Special Forces Group oriented itself toward Europe.

The A-Team was designed to function along lines similar to the techniques used by the partisan commands in Korea. Americans would work with bands of up to 1,500 fighters. To train and lead those partisans the US officers and noncoms needed to possess all the military skills present in a much larger organization. Intelligence, communications, weapons expertise, demolitions, and medical care were all required specialties. In addition, since men could be killed or incapacitated and not easily replaced, Special Forces very early began to cross-train its soldiers in other disciplines so an operator could step up to fill in for a fallen comrade. Depending on the popularity of Special Forces and the size of the US Army at different times, A-Teams have fluctuated in size from a half-dozen to fifteen operators, with a dozen (two officers plus ten noncommissioned officers) being the most typical size. At times when staffing was tight the problem of cross-training became particularly acute.

In June 1953 riots in East Germany suggested the possibility of more intense uprisings in Eastern Europe. The Tenth Group had finished its training and the Joint Chiefs of Staff had hashed out issues over its place in American war plans. The Tenth Group was posted to Bad Tölz, Germany, a month later. There it perfected its craft in maneuvers against the US Seventh Army—the American contribution to the North Atlantic Treaty Organization (NATO), created in 1947 to defend against a Soviet invasion of Europe—the forces of other NATO members, and in field exercises.

Tensions persisted between Special Forces and the conventionally trained combat commanders whose horizons ended with a vision of Soviet tanks flooding across the East German and Czech borders to attack NATO. The Special Forces received little support from Seventh Army brethren. Over time the strength of the Tenth Group tumbled by half. Under pressure from conventional commanders, with their desire for boots on the front lines, and without a practicable partisan resistance to organize, the Special Forces tended to drift more to Ranger-style missions, that is, the commando-type role, which had more appeal for NATO commanders. Special Forces trained with or engaged in exercises against foreign paratroops, rangers, commandos, and clandestine units of Germany, France, England, Norway, Greece, Spain, Italy, Turkey, Jordan, Saudi Arabia, Iran, and Pakistan.

Nevertheless the Special Forces concept had been established. Perhaps the concept had not flourished, but the force expanded. A new group formed at Fort Bragg, deployed to Hawaii, and after changes in name and base, wound up on Okinawa as the First Special Forces Group, focused on Asia and sending missions to Thailand, South Vietnam, South Korea, the Philippines, and Taiwan, where they helped train Rangers or unconventional warfare units in those lands. This expanded the Special Forces envelope, introducing a task that would become a mainstay of its activity. It was here, in the Pacific, that the shadow warriors first created "Mobile Training Teams" for these instructional missions.

The silent warriors who had left Fort Bragg were again replaced, by a re-formed Seventy-Seventh Special Forces Group. As the 1950s ended, Special Forces formed an experienced—typically ten years in service and with average age of about thirty—and well-trained corps of unconventional warfare specialists with a presence in both Europe and the Pacific. There were three Special Forces groups totaling roughly 2,000 soldiers. The air force maintained its Carpetbagger capability in the form of an air transport detachment, still under Heinie Aderholt, most recently distinguished by cooperating with a CIA covert operation in Tibet. The marines kept up a ranger capability with their Force Reconnaissance Battalions. The navy lagged behind somewhat, having permitted its frogman force to atrophy after the Korean War. But all that was about to change.

2

THE PARALLAX SHIFT

ABSTRACT

In the decade of the 1960s Special Operations Forces came into their own, fought a war, but also changed missions in important ways. The Army Special Forces established themselves in the public's consciousness for the first time. In South Vietnam Special Forces began by training Vietnamese troops and then progressively added new functions: mobilizing and leading tribal irregulars in the "Montagnard" program, supporting pacification efforts by means of civic action, recreating the Ranger mission of long-range patrolling, conducting cross-border scout patrols and raids, and attempting to free prisoners of war by striking prison camps. Special Forces ended the war as a strong element of the US military establishment. Along the way they earned the Green Beret.

Special Forces materialized during a period when US military doctrine was actually least favorable to their creation. Under President Dwight D. Eisenhower, who entered office near the end of the Korean War, the military's emphasis shifted from preparing its forces for near-term potential conflict to a sort of rolling target date receding into the future. The purpose of this measure had been to reduce defense spending by stretching out programs. Its concrete application lay in the doctrine known as "massive retaliation," unveiled publically by Secretary of State John Foster Dulles in early 1954, which emphasized threats of nuclear retaliation and the use of tactical nuclear weapons. Massive retaliation favored the navy and air force over the army, which contracted during the Eisenhower administration.

The struggle to adapt army forces for a nuclear warfare environment led to dedication of budget funds to the army's own tactical nuclear weapons. It also reorganized conventional units in a way that reduced their vulnerability to atomic attack but simultaneously limited their combat capability. These measures put a premium on front-line boots on the ground, within the framework of a smaller army, in effect erecting another obstacle to the expansion of Special Forces. In their efforts to remain relevant, Special Forces took on some very questionable roles, such as the mission of having individual operators drop behind enemy lines to place "atomic demolition munitions."

By the late 1950s a backlash had begun, with such prominent generals as Maxwell Taylor and James M. Gavin arguing that the army had become hollow, losing its capabilities to conduct both conventional and brush-fire—or counterguerrilla—wars. In running for the presidency in 1960, candidate John F. Kennedy accepted this critique and promised to rebuild America's capabilities across the full spectrum of warfare. President Kennedy's energy and support brought about marked changes for Special Forces. At the same time, international developments created demands that brought Special Forces to the foreground of US military endeavors.

How Did President Kennedy Change Special Forces?

President Kennedy showed himself to be very concerned about the ability of the United States to meet challenges at the brush-fire level, short of conventional war. Counterinsurgency became a watchword in the Kennedy administration. Indeed, at the topmost level of government Kennedy created a subpanel of his National Security Council, the Special Group (Counterinsurgency), specifically dedicated to monitoring US efforts in this field and providing impetus to new policy and technological initiatives. Kennedy aides encouraged the creation of a "counterinsurgency seminar" that would impart knowledge of the problems of brush-fire contingencies to officials across government, and the White House paid attention to its attendance and performance statistics. Kennedy aides, among them Walt W. Rostow, exhibited specific concern regarding Special Forces. Rostow spoke at the Special Warfare Center at Fort Bragg and arranged for President Kennedy to visit there.

John F. Kennedy went to Fort Bragg on October 12, 1961. The day is renowned in Forces' lore as the moment when Special Forces was awarded the Green Beret. Armies throughout the world distinguished themselves, and even their particular units, with berets of varied color and design, something the US military had resisted. From the early days of Special Forces the A-Teams had adopted "unauthorized" forms of headgear including (but not limited to) berets, but these had always been unauthorized. Theoretically a trooper could be disciplined for being caught wearing one. The exotic headgear had mostly been used away from base and the eyes of senior officers. By the time Kennedy came to Fort Bragg most Special Forces had the berets, still officially illegal. The top Special Forces commander, Brigadier General William P. Yarborough, took a chance and received his president and commander in chief wearing a green beret. Jack Kennedy, a twinkle in his eye, saw the hat and asked, "Those are nice. How do you like the Green Beret?" Yarborough replied, "They're fine, Sir. We've wanted them a long time." Upon returning from his trip President Kennedy sent a thank you message that said, "I am sure that the Green Beret will be a mark of distinction in the trying times ahead."[1]

Ever since then Army Special Forces have been known as the Green Berets. Not only did Kennedy officially approve them, he used nearly identical language in his memorandum. Air Force Special Forces soon followed suit and adopted berets for their unconventional warfare units. Later the Army Rangers would be distinguished by red berets. After 9/11 berets were adopted for all army forces, with certain combat arms identified by color like the Rangers and the Special Forces. Here the Green Berets made a naming and fashion statement for the entire US military.

But the armed services did more than change hats. President Kennedy's emphasis on limited wars and counter-insurgency led to a host of changes. Kennedy reprised his compliment to the Green Berets in an April 1962 letter "To the United States Army." The army got the message. Officials hastened to assemble and print a slick pamphlet, *Special Warfare, U.S. Army: An Army Specialty*, released shortly thereafter. Among other things the book reprinted the president's letter and Walt Rostow's speech at Fort Bragg, and had Secretary of the Army Elvis J. Stahr Jr. saying, "I expect commanders to draw upon this material in their training . . . for proficiency in Special Warfare is an indispensable requirement for the effective soldier and combat leader in today's Army."[2] Not to be outdone, the US Marines released their own selection of readings on counterinsurgency and guerrilla warfare.

The moment came when Special Forces, like US intelligence, could really be called a "community." The navy and air force both got serious about unconventional warfare. The seamen supplemented their underwater demolition teams with Sea, Air, Land, or SEAL teams, with one created on each coast in January 1962. In Florida, at Eglin Air Force Base, that service created a mixed attack-transport-military advisory capability in its 4400th Combat Crew Training Squadron, familiarly known as "Jungle Jim." It reprised the air commandos of Burma fame, forming the First Air Commando Wing, which traced its lineage directly to the World War II formation with this number. Both the wing and a Special Air Warfare Center were created at nearby Hurlbut Field in April 1962. The army and air force both established special warfare staff at the Pentagon level.

By far the largest personnel growth took place in the Green Berets. All three existing Special Forces Groups were built up to their full strengths of about 1,500 soldiers. Four new groups appeared, a new provisional group for the Far East (which would become Fifth Special Forces in Vietnam), the Eighth Group in Panama and oriented to Latin America, and at Fort Bragg the Third and Sixth Groups, focused on Africa and the Middle East respectively. New groups were also added to the Army Reserve and National Guard. To staff all these forces far more people were required. The Special Warfare School began to graduate many more volunteers ("wash out" rates fell from nearly 90 percent to about 70 percent), producing many more Green Berets—over three thou sand annually compared to about four hundred previously. For the first time, to meet its 1965 manpower goals Special Forces accepted army recruits on their first term of service. That meant the army stopped insisting that the Green Berets be composed entirely of highly experienced soldiers. Within a few years that standard had expanded further to include draftees. A Pentagon report to President Lyndon Johnson in early 1965 tabulated army special warfare forces at 11,343 as of November 30, 1964.

The original Green Beret concept of fomenting resistance to an occupying enemy also widened in the counterinsurgency era. Now Green Berets assisted host country armed forces to combat guerrilla threats by means calculated to win the hearts and minds of indigenous populations. The Berets already helped train foreign troop units and mobilize local fighters. Now they aimed to help increase the efficiency of governments. The idea of increasing public acceptance for a government through civil affairs became a new technique.

This meant improving village and regional infrastructures and local conditions by means of medical services and construction work. Psychological warfare efforts aimed to cement the public's support. Special Forces added civil affairs groups, psychological warfare battalions, and engineer detachments. Augmenting the intelligence resources necessary to serve this variety of missions brought the addition of intelligence detachments and radio spies, elements of the Army Security Agency, the army's radio intelligence service. The old Special Forces "group" suddenly morphed into a "special action force." Four groups—those focused on Asia, Latin America, Africa, and the Middle East—acquired this status.

Innovation did not confine itself to organizations. Special Forces interest resulted in the development of new techniques and technology as well. Not satisfied with standard US Army issue, Special Forces sought the best equipment for its operators. If that meant Swedish submachine guns, German-made hiking boots, or extra-large backpacks, so be it. Special Forces had the funds and outside-of-channels contracting authority to procure what they needed. Some of this stuff was quite exotic, such as the rocket belt that carried a Green Beret through the air to land in front of President Kennedy for the climax of his Fort Bragg visit. More practical was the technique evolved for an aircraft snatching a man from the ground without landing, an innovation of interest to both the Forces and the CIA. The SEALs developed underwater sleds capable of transporting a half-dozen swimmers. All were popularized in James Bond movies of the 1960s.

Probably the most remarkable Special Forces technology initiative was its early adoption of the Armalite AR-15 semiautomatic rifle, a lightweight but powerful gun. As the M-16, this became the standard weapon for the US armed forces during the later part of the Vietnam War. After teething troubles in Southeast Asia, it not only survived to become the service weapon for many armed forces and paramilitary groups across the globe, but remains today (in its M-4 variant) the regular armament of the US military, including Special Operations Forces.

What Happened in Vietnam?

American Special Forces first appeared in South Vietnam in the summer of 1957. From then until 1971 Green Berets were constantly on the scene there. It was in Vietnam, and during the war, that Green Berets entered the American popular consciousness. In 1965 journalist Robin Moore published *The Green Berets*, a novel representing Special Forces actions in only a slightly fictionalized way. Sergeant Barry Sadler, at home recuperating from Vietnam War wounds, wrote "The Ballad of the Green Berets," which sold a million records within two weeks of its release and became the top hit of 1966. Despite growing popularity the Berets continued to have a delicate relationship with the larger military. Army officials wanted to prosecute Moore for revealing classified information in his novel, though that bit of silliness ended when John Wayne bought the movie rights. The Pentagon began to appreciate the advantages of a film portraying the war in a favorable light amid growing antiwar protest in the United States. The army provided its full cooperation for the movie version of *The Green Berets*, which appeared in 1968 with Wayne as the lead character.

The first Green Berets went on assignment to train South Vietnamese Special Forces, which had been created as a unit to work directly for South Vietnamese president Ngo Dinh Diem. After that Americans cycled through South Vietnam, usually in numbers equivalent to an A-Team, to train Vietnamese army troops. When the Army of the Republic of Vietnam (ARVN) created a Ranger force, Green Berets trained that as well, establishing a steady presence for the first time.

But the Berets' actual fight in Southeast Asia took place in Laos. There, Special Forces began what would become their first signature involvement. It all started as another training mission, to supplement French training for the Laotian army. Because the French had the formal responsibility for this under the 1954 Geneva Accords, the United States could not send a normal advisory group. Instead Washington undertook to furnish "technical" training. Since Green Berets were experts in given operational specialties, they seemed the best fit, particularly because the men were to pose as civilian contractors and serve on six-month rotations, which meant that they did not have much time to acclimate. Stripped-down A-Teams of eight, including a motor mechanic (drafted in from the Eighty-Second Airborne Division because Special Forces did not possess this specialty), were sent direct from Fort Bragg. A dozen teams plus a B-Team control arrived in July 1959. They hired Thai interpreters to compensate for their lack of language proficiency and were farmed out to several Laotian army bases. About a hundred Special Force troops were involved.

A third rotation of Green Berets were in-country by August 1960, when a neutralist revolt within the Laotian army created a third side in the civil war. Washington allied with the anti-communist side in the fight, and the Berets began to work as military advisers rather than trainers. The first American casualties in this war came in March 1961 when communist Pathet Lao forces overran a Laotian infantry battalion that was accompanied by four Green Berets. Sergeants John M. Bischoff and Gerald M. Biber were killed, and their leader, Captain Walter H. Moon, was captured and executed several months later. One man escaped.

Special Forces' role changed again in the period from May 1961 to July 1962, when the Laotian sides were negotiating a new political settlement and a fragile ceasefire was in effect. A standard US military advisory group took up much of the training work, while Washington turned its gaze more and more toward South Vietnam. The North Vietnamese were beginning to infiltrate troops to the South down a network, soon dubbed the Ho Chi Minh Trail, that ran through the

Laotian panhandle. To disrupt that flow the Americans sought to recruit tribal irregulars in southern Laos. Special Forces, in a role akin to their concepts for working with partisans in Soviet rear areas, were well suited to train and command troops of this kind. Project "White Star" embodied this effort, led by Lieutenant Colonel Arthur D. ("Bull") Simons. The White Star teams were divided between service with Hmong and Kha tribesmen and Lao regular forces. Simons received his support from the CIA. The force gradually increased to 433 troops in the spring of 1962, but was withdrawn from Laos after new Geneva accords that summer.

By then Green Berets had begun regular service in South Vietnam. The ARVN had established its own Special Forces, to which Americans were attached, while ARVN Rangers trained at several bases, where they were helped by Green Berets. Special Forces also assisted the South Vietnamese militia known as the Civil Guard. The United States established a Military Assistance Advisory Group, succeeded by the Military Advisory Command Vietnam (MACV) in 1962. The command reserved its covert warriors for clandestine and paramilitary projects plus special units. These remained the core activities for Green Berets throughout the Vietnam War. One of the exotic outfits was the Air Force's Jungle Jim squadron. As of December 1961 the 1,209 personnel on secret warfare missions in South Vietnam exceeded regular American military strength, which then stood at 1,062.

Who Were the Montagnards?

The French word *montagnard*, literally one who lives in the mountains, became the colloquial term applied to a wide range of primitive tribesmen who inhabited the Central Highlands of South Vietnam. Informally called "yards," they became quite dear to Special Forces. It happened this way: in late 1961 a civilian humanitarian worker, concerned about the security of the tribes, approached a CIA deputy in Saigon. That man had charge of the agency's paramilitary effort in Vietnam, in effect controlling all Special Forces activities. He became convinced that the aid worker was right about the danger facing the tribes, and that South Vietnamese Rangers could not handle the problem. The better idea was to actually recruit and organize the tribes as irregular troops. That's where the Green Berets came in. They could do the training and organizing. The aid worker plus Central Intelligence Agency operatives approached a village where insurgents of the National Liberation Front had been extorting food and money. The Rhadé tribe agreed to participate. In February 1962 Captain Ron Shackleton with Team A-113 were taken to the area aboard a CIA aircraft and moved to the village, Buon Enao. They became the advance guard for the Berets' most ambitious effort to date.

The Montagnard project became an enormous success, replicated or supplemented in various ways throughout South Vietnam. The villages were endowed with local militias, while additional training and weapons armed tribesmen of "Civilian Irregular Defense Groups" (CIDGs), as the tribal units were called. From Buon Enao the concept was applied to more villages. From each the wave of security flowed outward. The best CIDGs were grouped into strike companies. Similar "mountain scouts" were recruited to screen the South Vietnamese side of the borders with Laos and Cambodia. In the lowlands river pirates, religious sects, and villages of the Cambodian ethnic minority were endowed with similar local militias. By the end of 1962 there were 1,500 "strikers" plus more than 10,000 tribal troops. A year later the militia numbered over 43,000 and the CIDGs some 18,000 strikers. The program had spread all across South Vietnam. It was a feather in Americans' caps.

Security represented only one part of the counterinsurgency concept. Tribal hearts and minds were to be won through various kinds of assistance projects, what Special Forces and its psychological warfare brethren knew as "civic action." A huge number of civic action projects were carried out by Green

Berets in South Vietnam. That tabulation includes nearly 50,000 economic aid projects, over 34,000 educational ones, a slightly greater number of welfare initiatives, and almost 11,000 medical projects. Berets exhibited enormous energy.

More Special Forces were necessary to run the American effort. In 1963 almost seven hundred Berets served in South Vietnam. Late the next year there were nearly one thousand Green Berets in-country just for the Montagnard program. Until September 1962 the A-Teams went to villages on temporary duty, but at that point, with burgeoning roles and missions, the army created a provisional unit, Special Forces, Vietnam. Two years later this was replaced by the Fifth Special Forces Group (Airborne), headquartered at Nha Trang. At the end of 1963 there were thirty-six A-Teams in the villages, four B Detachment command elements, and the C Detachment at Nha Trang. When the Johnson administration began sending US regular troops to the war, there were just two US ammunition stockpiles in the South and one of them, at Nha Trang, belonged to the Fifth Special Forces. The group became the Green Beret high command for the Vietnam War. By then the mountain campaign had assumed its classic shape.

National Liberation Front (NLF) guerrillas were not slow to recognize the Montagnard program as an emerging threat. In mid-1962 the NLF made its first significant attack on a yard village, against the Sedang tribe in the highlands. Driven off, they returned in greater force a couple of days later and thought they were teaching the tribe a lesson. Instead, enraged Sedang joined up in even larger numbers. The first pitched attack from the enemy came in January 1963 at Plei Mrong in Jarai tribal territory. The camp held out even though half its camp strike force was away on patrol. Green Beret captain Roger H. Donlon received the first Congressional Medal of Honor awarded in the Vietnam War for his defense of Nam Dong with Detachment A-726 in July 1964. Another Medal of Honor went to Lieutenant Charles Q. Williams for his July 1965 fight at Dong Xoai.

In these and other battles nearby South Vietnamese regular troops often did not respond to calls for help. The ARVN held large bases in the upland valleys and made big sweeps that rarely contacted the elusive NLF. Special Forces did much of the fighting. Their border surveillance posts and teams detected the enemy, and camp strike forces were the first to fight. Militias were consolidated into CIDGs, usually with several company-size units per Special Forces post. Camps would be assaulted. Quick reaction forces were clearly needed. The best strikers soon gathered in battalion-size Mobile Strike Forces, known as "Mike" Forces, controlled by the regional B Detachments. The Fifth Group formed a Mike Force Command as a general reserve. In search of even faster reaction times, the group established "mobile reaction forces" for each South Vietnamese corps area, and these evolved into additional Mobile Strike Force Commands. As airborne or air assault units they could join a fight by helicopter. South Vietnamese Special Forces held titular command of the camps. Their participation varied from place to place, sometimes leading, at other camps standing aside. Green Berets exercised a significant leadership role—and the Mike Forces were purely Americans leading indigenous fighters.

Possibly the biggest Green Beret headaches came precisely from the South Vietnamese. There was no love lost between South Vietnamese troops and the tribesmen. For years Saigon had acted with studied arrogance in the highlands. At one level the Special Forces mobilization of the tribes created a threat to Saigon's political control. Montagnard ethnic feeling increased as the tribes were armed and received military training. In the summer of 1964 a national unity movement started among the yards, and that September a number of camps rose in revolt. More than eighty ARVN soldiers died in the fighting that followed. Green Berets in some camps intervened to save their South Vietnamese counterparts, and it was a Special Forces officer who finally convinced the yards to end their revolt. Tensions persisted, and Saigon's cosmetic political concessions did not satisfy the Montagnard thirst for autonomy. Three years later the national unity group took to the bush, crossing the border into Cambodia, where Montagnards fought all comers. As for Saigon, when the United States began its withdrawal from the war, the South Vietnamese seized their first opportunity to terminate the CIDG program, designating all the Montagnard strikers as South Vietnamese Rangers. The Fifth Special Forces Group left South Vietnam in March 1971.

Green Beret efforts with the Montagnards—and in the earlier period with White Star in Laos—created many emotional ties and fond memories, but more important still, they shifted one pole of the overall Special Forces mission. Designed to work behind enemy lines to create a partisan resistance, the Green Berets now found themselves training and leading irregular troops in support of a US ally. Before Vietnam the Special Forces had done training too, but as a secondary mission beside its main role. After Vietnam, at least in peacetime, training indigenous forces became a primary role.

What Happened to the Rangers?

The Ranger units that had disappeared as the Korean War drew to a close returned during Vietnam. Part of the parallax shift of Vietnam involved not only the return of the Rangers but also the revamping of their role and its diffusion, creating a multiplicity of special operations units under different banners, and with different operating areas, but with similar purposes. The essential function became known as the "long-range patrol." The Rangers in Korea had done this but had not had the name. The long-range patrol became an accepted tactic in Vietnam. Long Range Patrol (LRP) companies were attached to divisions, as had been the case in Korea. The specialist fighters were known as "lurps." These elite troops typically worked in five-man patrols inserted into enemy-held territory, colloquially called "Indian country." Patrols would enter Indian country, sometimes on foot but usually by helicopter, and observe the adversary for periods of up to a week, calling in air strikes, artillery, or ground troops when they found suitable targets.

The Marine Corps built a similar capability into its Force Reconnaissance companies (descendants of the Marine Raiders of World War II fame), and again one was assigned to each division. Late in the war the lurp units of the US Army were regrouped into the Seventy-Fifth Infantry Regiment (Ranger), bringing back the storied name. The lurps and Force Recon Marines continued to serve the divisions to which they were assigned.

An important drawback of the lurp companies is that they were limited to the sectors of the divisions they served. The Military Assistance Command Vietnam (MACV) also needed this kind of capability for use on a regional basis. In the northern part of South Vietnam, controlled by the marines, the Third Force Reconnaissance Battalion met this challenge. Elsewhere in South Vietnam it was Special Forces that stepped up. To provide a theater-wide capability, in mid-1964 the Fifth Group created Project "Delta" around its B-52 detachment. Under Major Charlie Beckwith, Project Delta played an important part in 1965 battles. Delta give MACV the ability to move a lurp force anywhere in South Vietnam and saturate an area with scout patrols, then follow up. In 1966–67 the Fifth Group took a couple of B-Teams (B-50 and B-56), recruited numbers of South Vietnamese, and created Projects "Omega" and "Sigma," which worked for the corps commands. Unlike the lurps and Force Recon, purely US units, these were thousand-man forces only about a tenth of whom were American soldiers. Not only did Project Delta serve as prototype for these later additions, it would become the precursor for Special Forces' most famous unit.

What Was the "Green Beret Affair"?

At MACV insistence, in 1967 the Fifth Group set up Team B-57, Project "Gamma," as a purely US reconnaissance unit specifically aimed at investigating North Vietnamese activities in

Cambodia. Intelligence remained an important Special Forces function, and Gamma ran agent networks. Both the Military Assistance Command Vietnam and Washington were intensely concerned with the presence of Liberation Front and Hanoi troops in that neutral land. Project Gamma conducted patrols in addition to its agent networks. In 1969 Project Gamma's activities led to the biggest controversy of the war so far as Special Forces were concerned. In the "Green Beret Affair" an agent working for Gamma who was suspected of spying for the enemy died at the hands of his American handlers. General Creighton V. Abrams, MACV commander at the time, ordered a criminal investigation. Colonel John B. Rheault, the Fifth Group commander, tried to protect his men. Abrams held a jaundiced view of the Green Berets and was prepared to pursue the charges to the hilt. But the affair also implicated the Central Intelligence Agency—which apparently had approved the murder—as well as Special Forces, and the agency refused to cooperate with investigators or testify at courts-martial. In the end the Nixon administration quashed these proceedings. Nevertheless the affair ended Colonel Rheault's career.

What Was the Studies and Observation Group?

Aside from Project Gamma, Rangers and lurps mostly operated within South Vietnam. Forays into the hinterland were the métier of yet another unconventional warfare force, the innocuously named "Studies and Observation Group" (SOG). All the armed services participated in the Studies and Observation Group. They engaged in a covert campaign against North Vietnam, across the borders into Laos and Cambodia, and in Thailand helping the Thai with their own insurgency problem. SOG was active in South Vietnam too. As with the Montagnard program, this all began with the Central Intelligence Agency. In the very early days of the war the agency's Saigon station concentrated all its paramilitary activities into a unit called the "Combined Studies Group." One of those initiatives involved efforts to get back at North Vietnam by directly inserting agents and action groups. Green Berets were first drafted into this project as part of their mission of training South Vietnamese Special Forces. The covert program against the North utilized South Vietnamese facilities and drew on its unconventional warfare troops for training and for the crucial sea- and airborne missions to infiltrate commandos into the North.

American authorities were never satisfied with this program, which in its early years produced no results whatever. At the same time the CIA had discredited itself with its disastrous Bay of Pigs invasion of Cuba. President Kennedy ordered inquiries after that failure, and among the recommendations he approved was to take the paramilitary function away from the Central Intelligence Agency and give it to the military. In Vietnam this led to Operation Switchback, at the end of 1963, in which both the Montagnard program and the special warfare mission were taken over by the Pentagon. The Combined Studies Group became part of the MACV command, eventually supplanted by the Studies and Observation Group.

Final preparations for Switchback were underway when John F. Kennedy was assassinated in Dallas in November 1963. Something else happening simultaneously was a push to increase the effectiveness of Vietnam special operations by increasing American unilateral control. That move formed part of a White House directive in preparation at the very moment of Kennedy's assassination. The first big unilateral campaign, also then in planning, was a program of covert pressure against North Vietnam known as OPLAN 34-A. President Lyndon B. Johnson, Kennedy's successor, approved OPLAN 34-A in the first days of 1964. The Studies and Observation Group had its foundation stone in the 34-A operations.

Colonel Clyde Russell, first leader of the Studies and Observation Group, built a full-service unconventional warfare organization. There were ground (army), naval (navy/marine), and air (navy/air force) elements of the group. Five control elements combined to form the group. These dealt respectively with maritime operations, air support, psychological warfare, infiltration of North Vietnam (called "Footboy"), and cross-border operations. The SOG was and remained a supersecret entity, revealed on a strict need-to-know basis, storied and rumored even among other Green Berets. For example, the Fifth Special Forces Group published a monthly magazine in Vietnam called, naturally enough, *The Green Beret*. In thousands of pages of published material over the Vietnam years *The Green Beret* never mentioned the Studies and Observation Group, even though many Special Forces warriors passed on to its ranks.

Given its unconventional warfare purpose the group had a very unusual position within the US command structure. Though embedded within the Vietnam command, then under General William C. Westmoreland, the supremo had only the most general supervision over the group. Its reporting chain really ran to Washington, to the special warfare component of the Joint Chiefs of Staff, and through it, to the very top level of the US government. The 34-A schedules and, later, the lists of planned reconnaissance patrols, were approved by the Pentagon. The most important operations would be considered at the White House.

The navy and marines took the stage first, because the initial push with 34-A was to mount a series of coastal raids against the North. The SOG maritime element established a base at Da Nang on the central Vietnamese coast, where they were given a number of fast craft called "swift" boats or "nasty" ones depending on their class. Navy mechanics were drafted in to service the ships, while SEALs and marines of the Force Reconnaissance battalions (descendants of the Marine Raiders of World War II) planned the raids using CIA intelligence, with mission approvals from Washington. Most of the operations involved shooting up coastal targets or deceiving Hanoi by suggesting that partisan bands were infiltrating. Some sorties aimed to capture North Vietnamese sailors for questioning, leaving behind leaflets for psychological warfare purposes. Occasionally landing parties went ashore to sabotage North Vietnamese installations. Raids mounted from Da Nang in August 1964 played a role in the famous Gulf of Tonkin Incident, when timing of the 34-A missions simultaneously with the cruise of the US destroyer *Maddox* off North Vietnamese shores led Hanoi to believe both formed parts of the same operation.

Ground patrols began in the summer of 1964 with South Vietnamese–led forays into Laos from northernmost South Vietnam. Failure here quickly convinced American commanders that US-led cross-border operations were the way to go. By this time Colonel Donald D. Blackburn had taken up the SOG reins, and under him the unit assumed its final form. A training camp at Long Thanh, northeast of Saigon, became the avenue for Vietnamese and tribesmen to enter SOG units. The patrols would launch from "forward operating bases," the first of which were placed outside Da Nang and at Kham Duc Special Forces camp in the Central Highlands. It was SOG that, by capturing North Vietnamese equipment, brought in the first concrete evidence of Hanoi's regular army troops inside South Vietnam. Cross-border operations into Laos began with Project "Shining Brass" in 1965. Organized in "Reconnaissance Teams" of three Americans leading nine indigenous troops (these were informally called "spike" teams), SOG patrols headed for mission areas outside South Vietnam's borders. Aside from scout patrols the Reconnaissance Teams carried out missions to assess the damage inflicted by air strikes, particularly after B-52 "Arc Light" bombings; ones to place wiretaps on enemy phone lines; and others to free prisoners.

Master Sergeant Richard J. Meadows became the poster boy for SOG warriors. He brought his Reconnaissance Team Iowa back from every Shining Brass mission without loss and held the undisputed record for capturing enemy troops, returning with more than a dozen, including some taken inside North Vietnam. His take amounted to nearly a quarter of all the enemy soldiers SOG captured during the entire war. Regular army through and through, Meadows had no desire to be an officer and agreed only reluctantly when Westmoreland insisted on promoting him in the field. The SOG troops were a real elite—and on dangerous ground. The North Vietnamese closely observed the territory along the Ho Chi Minh Trail, and they had plentiful security troops. By one count 81 Americans, by another count 102, died in SOG cross-border operations. Total losses of the group were at least 300 Americans, including 57 missing in action. At least eight Green Berets with SOG earned Medals of Honor in Vietnam, all of them posthumous.

As with the CIDG program, SOG operators came to realize the need for quick reaction forces to reinforce threatened RTs or FOBs, screen conventional operations, or conduct special missions. In 1968, when the North Vietnamese assaulted Kham Duc, undoubtedly to eliminate it as a launch point, the need became blindingly apparent. Hornet Force platoons were the largest contingents at the time, perhaps fifty fighters intended for bigger missions on the lines of the OSS Operational Groups of World War II. Now Hatchet Forces were added, larger units capable of sustained fighting. They also engaged in classic commando-style activities, continuing to uphold the mantle of unconventional warfare.

A June 1967 strike that President Johnson personally approved pitted B-52 bombers and a Hatchet Force against a North Vietnamese base intelligence knew as "Oscar-8." The attack was quite dangerous because the Arc Light strike proved much less effective than anticipated and the enemy were in much greater strength than thought.

Possibly the most notable example of this type was Operation Tailwind, carried out in Laos in September 1970, one of three ops of this size. The Hatchet Force on this foray numbered sixteen Americans and 110 indigenous troops. Every American on the mission was wounded, along with nearly a third of the Montagnards, but they uncovered a North Vietnamese base camp, captured documents that detailed the workings of the Ho Chi Minh Trail, and diverted the enemy from attacking a CIA-led Hmong force to their south. Tailwind also illustrates another aspect of special operations: missions can become controversial even years later. In this case, nearly four decades afterward one of the SOG troopers told television journalists that sarin nerve gas had been used in the attack, setting off an intense public furor.

Colonel John K. Singlaub defended the operators, though this mission took place under his successor, noting that troops often used tear gas but never nerve agents. It was also demonstrable that the Hatchet Force had not had the hazmat suits standard when handling such agents, and that they had conducted no decontamination afterward—heading straight for a drink instead.

It was Singlaub who elevated SOG to its peak performance. At that point Studies and Observation Group aggregated roughly one thousand Americans and nine thousand Vietnamese or Montagnard personnel. Its ground forces included over five thousand Green Berets and indigenous troops in more than one hundred Recon Teams, over fifty Hornet Forces, seventeen Hatchet Forces, and two battalions. For psychological warfare purposes Singlaub moved ahead on a "Voice of Freedom" broadcast radio station located at Hue. Under him the cross-border program became robust enough to require a regional apparatus. Task forces akin to current Special Operations Command practice formed to conduct the missions. In Vietnam days these were called Command Control South, Central, and North, each responsible for that region of South Vietnam. The "Shining Brass" patrols into Laos, when their cover stories wore thin, were renamed "Prairie Fire." There were 563 of these patrols on Singlaub's watch, along with 139 Hornet Force operations. The SOG commander worked to improve radio communications with spike teams in the field by emplacing a repeater transmitter on a high peak in Laos to maintain contact.

Other efforts by Command Control North included "Nickel Steel," featuring forays into the Demilitarized Zone separating the zones of Vietnam; and "STRATA," lurp-style feelers into North Vietnam itself. Colonel Singlaub also terminated Project "Footboy," carried out directly by the SOG command. Its efforts to infiltrate North Vietnam had degenerated into deceptions designed to convince Hanoi that a resistance movement existed in the North, but the northerners had captured and often turned all the commando teams who were inserted. The Johnson administration also ended its bombing of North Vietnam when peace talks began at Paris, making it impossible for SOG aircraft to supply the commandos.

Meanwhile Command Control Center conducted patrols in the area where the borders of Vietnam, Laos, and Cambodia met, and Command Control South sent its teams into Cambodia, a project known as "Daniel Boone" and later "Salem House." There were 386 spike team insertions into Cambodia under Singlaub. The Reconnaissance Teams were smaller, but their purposes were the same. Prisoner liberation attempts were called "Bright Light" operations. There were forty-five of these missions in 1968. By then the Studies and Observation Group had created the basis for even greater levels of activity. There were just over a thousand Laos spike missions from then through the end of the program. At 1,449 there were nearly 50 percent more patrols into Cambodia, backed up by forty-three Hornet Force ventures and a dozen Hatchet Force operations.

Studies and Observation Group veteran—and expert— John L. Plaster exaggerates when he compares total North Vietnamese strength on the Ho Chi Minh Trail with the number of Green Berets in Command Control North to assert that every SOG American tied down a full battalion of the enemy. In Plaster's view this amounts to "the most successful economy of force [operation] in U.S. history."[3] His claim is misleading since North Vietnamese troops were engaged in logistics work, anti-aircraft defense against the American bombing, extending the

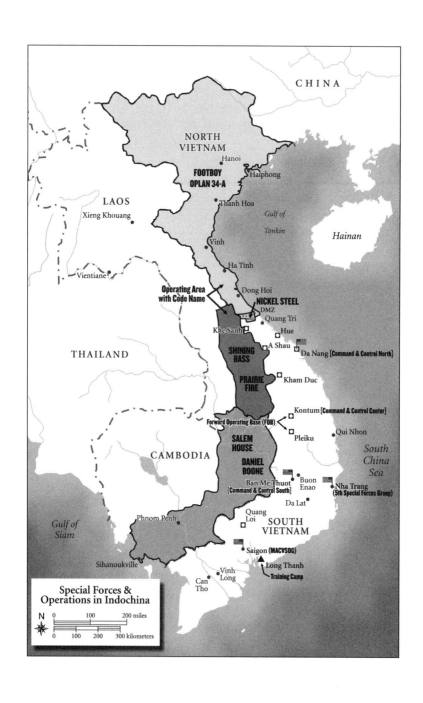

CHINA

NORTH
VIETNAM

Hanoi

FOOTBOY
OPLAN 34-A

Haiphong

LAOS

Xieng Khouang

Thanh Hoa

Gulf of
Tonkin

Hainan

Vinh

Ha Tinh

Vientiane

Dong Hoi

Operating Area
with Code Name

NICKEL STEEL

DMZ
Quang Tri

THAILAND

Khe Sanh

Hue

A Shau

Da Nang [Command & Control North]

SHINING
BASS

PRAIRIE
FIRE

Kham Duc

Kontum [Command & Control Center]

Forward Operating Base (FOB)

SALEM
HOUSE

Pleiku

Qui Nhon

South
China
Sea

CAMBODIA

DANIEL
BOONE

Ban Me Thuot
[Command & Control South]

Buon
Enao

Nha Trang
(5th Special Forces Group)

Da Lat

Phnom Penh

Quang
Loi

SOUTH
VIETNAM

Gulf of
Siam

Sihanoukville

Saigon **(MACVSOG)**

Long Thanh
Training Camp

Can
Tho

Vinh
Long

Special Forces &
Operations in Indochina

N
0   100   200 miles

0   100   200   300 kilometers

Trail, simply moving along it, and fighting in Laos itself; not to mention that plenty of Montagnards and South Vietnamese fought alongside the Americans, but Plaster's basic point is correct—that the Green Berets with SOG were among the most effective fighters in the Vietnam War.

What Was the Sontay Raid?

Known by the code name Operation Kingpin, this 1970 raid was undoubtedly the most ambitious Special Forces strike mission of the Vietnam War. It aimed at a target in the heart of North Vietnam, only a few miles outside Hanoi, and sought to free American prisoners, primarily navy and air force pilots, held by the North Vietnamese. A number of features distinguished Operation Kingpin from other unconventional warfare initiatives in the war.

In 1966 the Studies and Observation Group had added a Joint Personnel Recovery Center (JPRC), an element dedicated to liberating prisoners held by the enemy. The Recovery Center faced tremendous obstacles. The difficulty looming over its work was the intelligence gap. Intelligence on prisoners held by the enemy was always imprecise and mostly dated, making it difficult to craft concrete plans. The first big mission proved a costly failure. Rather than target raids the rescuers next shifted to a strategy of mounting raids into sectors that *might* contain prisoner camps. Before the Sontay mission the Joint Personnel Recovery Center had made more than ninety rescue attempts. Though remains of American soldiers were recovered, and a number of South Vietnamese freed, the only American prisoner to return was Sergeant Nick Rowe, a Special Forces adviser who had been captured in 1963. But Rowe had escaped by himself and been picked up by air cavalry troops, not freed by a JPRC mission. The Sontay raid would be different.

The US air campaign against the North periodically resulted in warplane losses and known American prisoners.

More than 350 Americans were being held in North Vietnam when the bombing stopped. Photo reconnaissance eventually identified a compound outside Sontay, not far from Hanoi, as a camp housing perhaps fifty to sixty American prisoners. By the spring of 1970 the information was concrete enough that Brigadier General Donald Blackburn, the Joint Chiefs' special warfare assistant, could ask for a rescue feasibility study. In August, after approval of the concept, a joint task force formed to carry out the mission. Rather than utilize SOG or the JPRC, the operation was organized from outside of South Vietnam. This reflected the desirability of launching the raid from Thailand, enabling the force to enter North Vietnam through the back door, so to speak, where it would face fewer air defenses. In addition, rehearsals for the mission, for security reasons, had to take place in the United States. Avoidance of South Vietnam also reduced the chance of any leak from the many Vietnamese associated with the Studies and Observation Group, who presumably included some enemy agents.

Air force special operations chief Brigadier General Leroy J. Manor became the task force commander and, under him, Colonel Bull Simons of the Green Berets was deputy. Captain Richard Meadows, the SOG maven, led a special team that would land inside the compound. The actual troop commander was Lieutenant Colonel Bud Sydnor, who selected the volunteers and rehearsed them beginning on August 20. The White House approved the raid in early October, and the force began its move to Thailand on November 10. In the meantime the navy planned a set of air attacks around Hanoi to distract the North Vietnamese while the raid was in progress. President Richard Nixon gave his final approval on November 18. By that time all the forces were in place. The navy's diversions were completely successful.

Two air force C-130 planes, very capable four-engine transports with advanced navigation gear, led the air formation to Sontay. Bull Simons's operators were aboard five large HH-53 helicopters and one HH-3, intended to land inside the compound and confound the North Vietnamese. Five A-1 "Skyraider" fighter-bombers went along to furnish close air support. The force left bases in Thailand in the evening of November 20. They refueled in the air and approached Hanoi without incident. But in the dark of night the choppers approached the wrong compound. Some pilots realized the error and moved on to the correct target. Two ships, including Colonel Simons and Sydnor's command party, landed at the wrong place. They regrouped to the correct compound, which, in the meantime had been taken down by Dick Meadows and his raiders.

Kingpin proved completely successful except that the raiders found no prisoners. Within ten minutes of landing a search team had determined that the compound was empty, at least of prisoners. The North Vietnamese had moved the prisoners elsewhere some time previously, and US intelligence never discovered that maneuver. Vice Admiral William McRaven, the planner of the Osama bin Laden raid (see the prologue), had previously made a study of Sontay as part of a review of special operations. He pronounces Kingpin "the best modern-day example of a successful special operation," and McRaven concludes it "should be considered textbook material for future missions."[4] This seems exaggerated in that no one was, in fact, rescued, and also because of the errors made by the helicopters carrying the raiders. Air Force Special Forces have been important parts of our unconventional warfare armada, and it is to them we now turn.

3

EBB AND FLOW

ABSTRACT

Like the army, the navy and air force multiplied their unconventional capabilities for Vietnam. After the stresses of the war, US economic problems along with the military's post-Vietnam restructuring and the traditional animosities between regular and unconventional warfare officers resulted in a considerable shrinkage of Special Forces. But the forces, now a community, and having demonstrated their utility in unmistakable terms, were considerably better prepared to persevere through a time of challenge. Unlike the aftermaths of previous conflicts, following Vietnam there could be no question of dismantling Special Forces, which indeed acquired a new identity as "Special Operations Forces." The rise of terrorism provided a new challenge and a new mission and resulted in the beginnings of a resurgence of the genus. The attempt to rescue Americans held prisoner in the Iran hostage crisis, though the operation itself failed, triggered the move to recreate the full spectrum of capabilities the Special Operations Forces had had in Vietnam.

The world of Special Forces expanded, perhaps exponentially, during the 1960s. Green Berets got most of the attention, but much of what they did—especially with the Studies and Analysis Group—would have been impossible without the unconventional warriors of the air force and navy. The

idea that a "community" of special operators exists origi-
nated around this time. The special warfare community
would march together into the future. But at the height of the
Vietnam War the warriors had little notion of the challenges
facing them.

How Did Air Force Special Warfare Evolve?

Air force had continued its special duty flight of transport
planes with the Twenty-First Troop Carrier Squadron, during
Korean War days familiarly known as the "Kyushu Gypsies."
The unit later moved to Okinawa and, when C-130 aircraft
began rolling off the production lines in the late 1950s, some
went to the Gypsies. At a stroke this development virtually
quadrupled the distance over which clandestine air missions
could be carried out. After tours with the CIA and with psychological warfare headquarters in Europe, Heinie Aderholt,
perhaps the single most important figure in the evolution of
air force unconventional warfare, returned to the Gypsies as
a major, leading its special operations detachment. With the
air force's blessings he supported CIA operations in Tibet and
Thailand. With the advent of the C-130 the air force had a capability for long-range covert missions.

Short hops into primitive airfields, which would charac-
terize the air effort in Southeast Asia, were a different matter. In the late 1950s the air force introduced its twin-engine
C-123 "Provider," but that went to standard transport squadrons. The army was developing the C-7 as a short-haul light
transport. The Provider could carry a bigger load but lacked
the short-takeoff-and-landing capacity of its competitor.
Conditions in Vietnam and Laos demanded aircraft capable
of taking off and landing in these short spaces. In 1962 the air
force deployed a Provider version modified for this. Colonel
Aderholt took a hand too. During the interval he was assigned
to the air branch of CIA paramilitary operations staff, Aderholt
had learned of a new single-engine plane that could be ideal.

He pressed for adoption of the HelioCourier and succeeded (CIA knew this craft by one name [L-28], the air force by another [U-10]). These three aircraft became mainstays of the air wing within the Studies and Observation Group as well as the CIA proprietary Air America. The war, particularly in Laos, could not have been conducted without them.

Combat capability began with the "Jungle Jim" unit. Partly a result of the air force responding to President Kennedy's demands, and partly to the service's dawning awareness that the US military as a whole was reconfiguring itself for counterinsurgency, chief of staff General Curtis E. LeMay moved ahead smartly. Identified with high technology throughout his career, here, in 1960, LeMay approved a unit outfitted with prop-driven T-28 fighter-bombers and B-26 light bombers. This was deliberate. Rapidly transitioning to supersonic aircraft, the air force realized that slow-flying prop planes would have more time to spot targets and strike them.

The innocuous 4400th Combat Crew Training Squadron ran its flag up at Auxiliary Field No. 9 of Eglin Air Force Base, Florida, in April 1961. At the time, Hurlbut Field, as it was renamed, consisted of wood-frame single-story barracks, plus sheds left over from World War II. It is today the headquarters of the Air Force Special Operations Command, descendent of the Special Air Warfare Center created there—and rivaling Fort Bragg as an unconventional war mecca—in 1962. Soon enough Jungle Jim left for South Vietnam, where it was given the code name Farm Gate and stationed at Bien Hoa. Officially the aircraft trained crews for the South Vietnamese air force. In actuality they flew strike and bombardment missions, with American pilots accompanied by South Vietnamese observers.

In Laos the strike capability began with Project "Mill Pond," a CIA operation utilizing B-26 bombers with air force crews seconded to the agency and flying in civilian clothes The ubiquitous Aderholt organized Mill Pond too. And when he returned to the United States, promoted colonel, this officer briefly commanded the First Air Commando Wing, the air force's initial venture with a full-scale counterinsurgency unit, along the lines of those who'd flown in Burma during World War II. Wing mixed together fighter-bombers, transports, and liaison aircraft, and it became the parent organization for Farm Gate.

A major innovation of air force special warfare during the Vietnam War was the gunship. This was a large aircraft—the C-47 would be the first used, followed by the C-119 and then the C-130—providing a stable platform for side- and/or front-firing heavy weapons and cannon, soon supplemented by electronic systems for targeting. The early C-47 version got the nickname "Puff the Magic Dragon." When these aircraft entered the force they went to the First Wing. More advanced planes joined the Fourteenth and Twenty-Fourth Wings. All of them were redesignated special operations wings in 1968. The gunships were especially effective in helping to defend outposts or patrols that were under attack, and in armed reconnaissance missions along the Ho Chi Minh Trail. The gunships became established elements of air Special Forces. By 1966 there were six thousand men and 550 aircraft assigned to air special operations.

What about the Navy?

Like the other armed services the navy, too, heeded President Kennedy's call. The chief of naval operations at the time, Admiral Arleigh Burke, recommended formation of the special units in March 1961. Early the next year the navy expanded its special warfare capability, formally creating the SEALs. Drawing on combat swimmers from the Underwater Demolition Teams, it created SEAL units called "teams." Team One, based at Coronado, California, would conduct Pacific operations, and Team Two, at Little Creek, Virginia, ones in the Atlantic. The first SEALs arrived in South Vietnam in March 1962. This branch's initial combat missions came there, collecting beach and hydrographic data along the coast. SEALs were based at the Naval Support Activity Da Nang and soon tapped by the CIA to support its agent infiltration into North Vietnam. Subsequently the SEALs supported the 34-A covert pressure program against the North, and they became a mainstay of the Maritime Branch of the Studies and Observation Group. As part of a Naval Advisory Detachment they helped train Vietnamese of the Coastal Security Service and plan its sorties off the northern coast. Project "Plowman," the group's maritime harassment program against the North, relied upon American sailors to maintain the boats and SEALs for their special warfare expertise. The navy unconventional warriors were important also for rescue missions and certain scout forays along the Cambodian coast.

With the SEALs' growing role came new capabilities. The underwater delivery vehicle was perfected by the mid-1960s and Special Boat Units evolved to handle this part of the mission. The North Vietnamese coast beckoned. In late 1967 the Joint Chiefs of Staff considered a scheme to block North Vietnam's Haiphong Harbor by scuttling a vessel in its main shipping channel. This concept, Operation Night Bolt, would have involved landing SEALs on nearby offshore islands. At some point it became clear that, while the navy had underwater delivery vehicles for the men, it lacked a vessel to get a SEAL strike force to the target in a covert fashion. Submarines were perfect for the task but, while they could carry the sailors, they had no means of actually launching a mission while remaining submerged. In November 1967 the navy began converting the sub *Grayback*, originally designed to carry a large-size cruise missile called the Regulus, and which therefore had a big shed on her deck. The shed was ideal to house swimmer delivery vehicles and, with bunk space instead of her missile gear, *Grayback* could carry up to sixty-seven SEALs. The boat was ready by the summer of 1968. She would be used once for a SEAL combat mission in Vietnam. That came in June 1972, as part of Operation Thunderhead, an attempt to rescue American prisoners believed to be escaping from a North Vietnamese prison. The *Grayback* launched her combat swimmers for a preliminary reconnaissance, but strong currents plus navigation errors sent them off course, and the mission was aborted. The delivery vehicle had to be abandoned when its battery power became exhausted, and the SEALs were rescued by a navy surface ship. The mission leader, Lieutenant Melvin S. Dry, was lost when he drowned while a helicopter was trying to return them to the submarine. Meanwhile the escaping prisoners were recaptured by the North Vietnamese.

Lieutenant Dry became one of forty-eight SEAL deaths in the Vietnam conflict. By far the majority of them occurred in the Mekong Delta and Rung Sat swamp, the southern part of the land, where SEALs participated in a sustained ground campaign. The fabled Rung Sat, which translates as "Swamp of the Assassins," had long been a wild bandit zone, now become a Liberation Front stronghold. A strong pacification effort began there in 1967. SEALs were perfectly adapted for this environment. Platoons of SEAL Team One set up there, and moved to new bases along the Mekong and Bassac Rivers. There they made ground patrols and sudden raids in support of navy riverine forces interdicting the waterways.

The most famous (or infamous) of these—another example of the propensity for special operations to become controversial years afterward—took place on February 25, 1969, when Delta Platoon of Team One under Lieutenant Bob Kerrey entered the village of Thanh Phong in search of a Liberation Front official. They left behind twenty-one civilian dead with no enemy captured. More than three decades later Kerrey, by then a university president and former US senator, who received a Medal of Honor for this raid, would be strongly criticized on suspicion of having perpetrated a war crime.

Pacification commanders also relied upon SEALs— and Force Recon marines—to lead the so-called Provincial Reconnaissance Units (PRUs) in this region. The PRUs were the strike teams of the "Phoenix" program, which aimed at the Liberation Front's infrastructure. Enemy cadres were to be "neutralized," either by arrest or elimination. The Phoenix program became contentious because of the perception it was an assassination machine. Opinions divided on the impact of Phoenix, and it led to more erosion of political support for the Vietnam War in the United States, but the SEALs had no part in that. They were very effective leaders of these unconventional PRUs. The SEALs received three Presidential Unit Citations for their actions in Vietnam, and these warriors earned three Medals of Honor, two Navy Crosses, plus forty-two Silver and 402 Bronze Star medals.

How about Elsewhere? Che Guevara?

As the Vietnam War continued and drew toward its end, Green Berets carried out their other missions worldwide. They added a new function too—conducting tests of the security of US facilities by masquerading as an enemy. Then they were drafted as emergency augmentation teams for US embassies. For example, during "Black September" in 1970, when airliners were hijacked to Jordan, and in 1973, when a terrorist organization calling itself "Black September" assaulted the Saudi embassy in the Sudan, killing two senior US diplomats, Green Berets reinforced the marine guards at the embassies in Amman (Jordan) and Khartoum (Sudan). But by far the best-known Special Forces operation of the era was its role in the death, in Bolivia in 1967, of the Argentinian revolutionary Che Guevara.

The Eighth Special Forces Group, responsible for Latin America, had been especially active. Nearly five hundred mobile training teams or assistance missions were dispatched to our southern neighbors during that decade. Working with embassies, Military Advisory Groups, and aid officials of the Alliance for Progress, they built clinics, opened mountain roads, helped improve local communications networks—all part of civic action—and trained troops, more than 100,000 over the period. During the peak year of 1965, 41,000 Latin American soldiers received Green Beret training.

In the spring of 1967 guerrilla bands began to harass *campesinos* in the countryside of Bolivia. The CIA soon suspected Cuban involvement, and intelligence connected Ernesto ("Che") Guevara, who had been allied with Fidel Castro since the Cuban Revolution, with the Bolivian troubles. That spring an American general sent to survey conditions in Bolivia reported back that the Bolivian government especially wanted help creating an elite ranger unit to combat the guerrillas. Special Forces sent a training team under Major Ralph Shelton to drill the Bolivians that became the Second Ranger Battalion. In October, just a few weeks after finishing their course, the Bolivian Rangers stumbled into Che's band and, after a firefight, captured him. The Bolivians executed Guevara a few days later. Walt Rostow, by that time national security adviser to President Johnson, extolled the mission to LBJ as an exemplar of Special Forces' work. Indeed the Che coup would be what people remembered about Green Berets in Latin America.

What Tensions Existed between Special Forces and the Conventional Military?

Conventional forces, not just the Berets, earned plenty of kudos in Vietnam. But a good argument could be made that special operations had fully proved their worth during the war. Yet tensions persisted between the unconventional warriors and their regular brethren. These can be traced to several sources. One was military budgets. Rising inflation, an economic downturn, plus the cost of the conflict absolutely required reductions in US defense spending. It is not often noted, but is nevertheless true, that the need to reduce the Pentagon budget played a significant role in Washington's withdrawal from South Vietnam. The generals, given the choice between losing big slices of combat capability such as infantry divisions, or cutting at the margin, choose the margin every time.

And Special Operations Forces were at the margin. Between 1969 and 1974 four of the seven Army Special Forces Groups were deactivated or moved to the reserves, one of them the unit responsible for the Che Guevara mission. The navy cut its SEALs by half, and the air force reduced its capability more than that, shrinking two wings into squadrons within the First Special Operations Wing, the one big formation it retained. The four-engine C-130 transports that had been its SOG heavy lifters were reassigned to the Tactical Air Command. The air force viewed special operations as a drain on its resources. By 1980 there would be fewer active service Green Berets than in the Fifth Group alone at the height of Vietnam, and in all the armed services about the number the army had had in 1969.

One driver in the Pentagon's decisions was the military's distaste for any more wars like Vietnam. In the 1970s counterinsurgency was viewed as a distraction from the mission of fighting a Russian enemy in Europe. Combat capability meant conventional force, to which the unconventional warriors contributed little. The army's Tenth Special Forces Group came home from Bad Tölz, Germany, leaving in place only one of its battalions, the equivalent of a 250-man infantry company. Even those Special Forces groups that were preserved were allowed to fall below strength. Some of the brass may have regretted these reductions, but there was general agreement on strengthening conventional forces in Europe, including designing and building an expensive new generation of combat vehicles. Funding for Special Forces declined 90 *percent* between 1969 and 1975.

Moreover, special operations strength was misleading, since it was not simply a matter of the number of Green Berets. The Army Rangers comprised two battalions by late 1974. In fact the sole force increase over the period would be addition of the second Ranger battalion—not coincidentally, a combat *unit.* Stanley McChrystal, whom we shall meet again later, graduated West Point in 1976 and took Ranger training. He would be drawn away to the paratroops, then the Green Berets, but dreamed of actually serving in a Ranger formation. "Following

Vietnam," McChrystal recalls of service at that time, "the Army was so broken that it wanted to make two perfect battalions whose excellence could then seep into the rest."[1]

On an equally personal level, combat arms officers harbored a certain resentment of the unconventional warriors. However excellent the fighters were, they had a freewheeling style and a tendency to get around regulations. With their direct channels to higher authorities, Special Forces leaders often succeeded in reversing orders given them by the regular chain of command. The poster episode for this kind of situation is probably the crisis between Vietnam boss Creighton Abrams and Green Beret leader Robert Rheault over the "Green Beret Affair."

Another major sore point was the persistent view that Special Forces diluted the quality of the regular military by siphoning off many of the best officers and noncommissioned officers. Nonconventional troop units had been abolished after World War II and Korea—and in the latter case the regulars had gotten their way, with the Ranger-trained specialists assigned to conventional units. One effect the prowess of Special Operations Forces in Vietnam did have was to make it impossible for the enemies of Special Forces to terminate them once again, but it did not prevent conventionally minded Pentagon leaders from minimizing Special Forces' role. The persistence of arguments against Special Forces remained perplexing.

It had been a standard tease in Special Forces that Green Beret officers never made general. That was wrong but also partly right. William Yarborough, who won the Green Beret, made general's rank, but he had risen through the ranks of the paratroops and was an intelligence specialist. Donald Blackburn, mastermind of the Sontay raid, became a general, possibly the first special warfare officer to do so. None of the commanders of the Fifth Special Forces in Vietnam or of the Studies and Observation Group held general's rank at the time, and fewer than half of them attained that rank later. The most famous would be John K. Singlaub, the SOG chief. In 1970 the commander of Army Special Forces was Major

General Edward M. Flanagan Jr. He was an airborne artillery officer, not a Green Beret, and would leave to lead the First Infantry Division. Flanagan viewed the future of Special Forces as centered on its mobile training and in the Ranger mission—long-range penetration patrols.

Why Did Special Forces Go into Decline after Vietnam?

To the traditional animosities between Special Forces and regular troops can be added the military spending issues of the time and the preference for "real" forces to fight a Big War. But the distaste for "another Vietnam" seems paramount. Far from John F. Kennedy's intention to make counterinsurgency a standard focus for the US military, the term almost disappeared from the lexicon. In 1967 the army had established a different doctrine, publishing a field manual on "stability operations." As the name suggests, this approach put the main emphasis on the efforts of large units. The residual mission for special warfare would be relegated to the category of "internal defense and development." Few officers or ambitious noncoms saw a career in that—Che Guevara or not—so there were fewer volunteers for the groups. Counterinsurgency even disappeared as a subject from the curricula of training courses. The former Special Warfare Center would be renamed the John F. Kennedy Center for Military Assistance. Special Operations Forces were increasingly reduced to the stalwarts of the sixties serving out their careers in the branch they loved. But—and this marked a sea change from the aftermaths of previous wars—Vietnam had made Special Operations Forces a true military component. There could be no question of abolishing the unconventional warfare community.

What Is Low-Intensity Conflict?

But the phenomenon of revolution, often taking the form of insurgency or subversion, did not evaporate regardless of whether the US military taught the subject. In Angola, Mozambique,

Rhodesia, Namibia, Western Sahara, Colombia, the Philippines, guerrilla wars persisted through the 1970s. There was an actual probability of dying in these revolutionary conflicts, compared to conventional war, where there were no such operations in progress and no possibility of becoming a casualty. Soldiers who were excited by action began to gravitate toward the Special Forces. The thinkers among them realized that the tactics and techniques for pursuing counterinsurgency needed to cover more than internal defense. In 1971 a British brigadier, Frank Kitson, published a book called *Low Intensity Operations*, a work that joined the pantheon of classic counterinsurgency texts. Transported to the American milieu, this became "low-intensity conflict" and the concept came to subsume many of the unconventional warfare elements that were Special Forces business.

Meanwhile the SEALs held on by the skin of their flippers. Air force special operations, reassigned to the Tactical Air Command, which remained dominated by a mafia of jet fighter pilots who had risen through the Vietnam air campaigns, had held on too. It had even developed a new capability—unconventional warriors akin to the army's old airborne "pathfinders," airmen who would drop in to a target ahead of mission aircraft and mark it for aircraft landings, the insertion of troops, or be ground observers guiding air strikes. These warriors would not get their name of "Special Tactics Units" until the 1980s—at this time they were known simply as "Brand X"—but they already had the capacity to work alongside Navy and Army Special Forces. With the new units came new terminology, reflecting more closely the multiservice nature of the troops, no longer known simply as Special Forces but as "Special Operations Forces," the name that is familiar today.

Did Rising Concern about Terrorism Influence SOF Trends, and When Did the Change Take Hold? What Is Delta Force?

One variety of low-intensity conflict was terrorism. Beginning in the mid-1970s, countering terrorism provided fresh purpose for Special Forces, a new role well suited to its elite warriors.

The development of units and tactics dedicated to this role fueled such force growth as did occur in the United States at the time. Airplane hijackings, the Black September incident, and the activities of the terrorist organization that took the name "Black September" and carried out murderous attacks against Israeli athletes at the 1972 Summer Olympics in Munich drew attention to the problem. The incoming administration of President Jimmy Carter determined to forge a capacity to deal with terrorist activities. Carter administration proclivities were reinforced by a March 1977 incident in Washington, DC, itself, where Muslim militants seized three buildings, including Washington's city hall and a 150 hostages. A subsequent siege lasted several days and ended with two dead and others wounded, including future mayor Marion Barry, who was shot in the chest.

Responding to presidential initiative, in November 1977 the army established a new formation called First Special Forces Operational Detachment Delta (SFOD-Delta). Colonel Charles R. Beckwith got the assignment to set it up. Beckwith, known in the army as "Chargin' Charlie," had led the similarly named Project Delta of the Fifth Special Forces in Vietnam. He figured he would need two years to bring the new Delta Force to combat readiness. As a stopgap measure Green Beret commander Major General Jack Mulhill ordered the Fifth Group, now under Colonel Robert Mountel, to form an ad hoc commando-style unit. Mountel called it "Blue Light." In what amounted to a parody of the long-standing resentment between conventional and special forces, some Green Berets argued that Delta siphoned the best men away from Special Forces and sought to abolish it in favor of Blue Light. Under the gun to prove his unit's capability, Charlie Beckwith managed to prepare his troopers quickly enough to pass a unit certification exercise in the summer of 1978. White House officials and army brass came down from Washington to witness the event. At that point the brass threw its weight behind Delta, and Blue Light did not survive. Ever since, the Delta Force has been a major component of Army Special Forces.

What Does Iran Have to Do with Special Forces?

The Iranian hostage crisis of 1979–81 would be the catalytic moment for the new missions of US Special Operations Forces. A tidal wave of religious and political fervor rose in Iran in the late 1970s that led to the overthrow of Shah Mohammed Reza Pahlavi, a hereditary monarch but a ruler who long before had been driven from power then reinstalled courtesy of a 1953 CIA covert operation. Iranians hated the shah for his autocratic and dictatorial ways. In early 1979 the shah's regime ended in an Islamic uprising. The deposed potentate sought refuge in Egypt, then Panama, but suffered from cancer and sought medical treatment in the United States. When he entered the United States, the Iranian capital, Tehran, exploded in fresh mass protests by Iranian students and Islamic militants, and on November 4, 1979, they took over the US embassy, capturing sixty-six American diplomats, CIA officers, and marine guards, most of whom they held hostage for fourteen months (fourteen women, African Americans, and a sick diplomat were released). Their captors demanded the shah be returned to Iran for trial.

President Jimmy Carter negotiated for release of the American hostages, but in a parallel effort he ordered preparations for a rescue attempt to be conducted by Special Operations Forces. The events of the hostage rescue set the future course of America's unconventional warriors.

What Happened in Operation Eagle Claw?

Code-named Operation Eagle Claw, the hostage mission bears many similarities to the Sontay raid of the Vietnam War. Washington began considering a rescue plan as soon as information became available (in this case the embassy takeover). The Pentagon cobbled together an impromptu joint task force to craft the plan and conduct the mission. It was clear from the beginning that only helicopters were capable of spiriting away the hostages and raiders quickly enough to avoid being overwhelmed by the Iranian militants. The question of precise intelligence regarding the location of the prisoners was paramount, but there were many other elements of intelligence that were instrumental to a successful rescue attempt. The secrecy of the mission had to be preserved so as to minimize incentives for the Iranian captors to move their prisoners elsewhere. The entire operation had to be planned, organized, rehearsed, and carried out on an urgent basis. Aerial refueling proved a key constraint. Fewer than half of the MC-130E "Combat Talons" left in the air force's inventory had that capability, necessary for the mission. All these things replicated the experiences of Kingpin, the Sontay raid.

The American raiders would be from the Delta Force. Air Force general James B. Vaught led the joint task force. Accounts by Colonel James H. Kyle, the air force's on-scene commander, and by Colonel Charles Beckwith, make clear that the rescue plan itself was concocted in a matter of days after the embassy takeover. Very quickly the plan, closely supervised by Joint Chiefs of Staff chairman General David C. Jones, centered on a Delta Force takedown followed by a helicopter extraction. The choppers needed to be launched from outside of Iran. For diplomatic and security reasons they would best be flown from a US Navy ship, in this case the aircraft carrier *Nimitz*. Tehran lay behind the range of the helicopters, even with extra fuel tanks and not bearing a load of heavily armed soldiers. Weather conditions, especially air temperatures, also critically affected helicopter range. This dictated an intermediate stop. American intelligence experts and operational planners scoured Iran maps and satellite photos for a suitable location. Taking control of an existing airfield would alert the Iranians to an incursion. Planners decided that a deserted space in the desert south of Tehran offered the best possibility. The choppers would fly there and be refueled from aviation gas brought in by MC-130 aircraft, which would also deploy a security force of Rangers to guard the site plus the Delta Force raiders and Colonel Beckwith. The navy and marines selected expert helicopter crews and the air force experienced plane drivers, and they practiced all aspects of the mission with Delta's operators using facilities in the United States.

For the concept to work, the temporary base, dubbed "Desert One," would have to be able to bear the weight of the loaded MC-130s as well as the helicopters. The CIA conducted a covert air mission to that site on March 30, 1980, carrying air force major John T. Carney plus agency experts, to survey the location, collect soil samples, and emplace a set of infrared landing strip lights that subsequent pilots could use to land. Meanwhile, distances and aircraft speeds made it impossible for the mission to be carried out within the space of a single night, requiring a layover of some kind. Planners chose to frame the mission with the assault force moving up to a hideaway site very close to Tehran, Desert Two, where the operators and helicopters would be concealed through the next day. After sunset the Delta Force men would drive into Tehran in trucks. Beckwith selected Major Richard Meadows, of Vietnam fame, now retired but a key Delta consultant, to personally travel to Tehran, scout the embassy, find the hiding place, and rent trucks for the raiders. Assisted by a couple of other Special Forces operatives infiltrated into Tehran in late April, Meadows would grease the rails and send an all-clear message when Operation Eagle Claw was poised for implementation.

Delta Force troopers would overcome the Iranian militants and free the hostages. The idea was that the helicopters would land, pick everybody up and fly on to an airbase that US Rangers would meanwhile have invaded and secured. Everyone would pack onto big C-141 transport planes to leave Iran. On the night of April 24 President Carter gave final approval. Delta Force, Rangers, and air force mission elements already deployed forward swung into action. The *Nimitz* launched the helicopters. One ship suffered a mechanical failure and had to scrub the mission. Several hours into their flight the choppers, over the Iranian desert, encountered a haboob, a violent dust storm, then another one. A second helicopter, its navigation systems affected, returned to the ship; while a third one had critical damage but continued to Desert One. At Desert One Colonel Kyle determined that the damaged chopper could not continue the mission, which put the force below the necessary minimum of six helicopters. Kyle informed General Vaught of the problem and the latter told the White House. President Carter approved Vaught's decision to shut down the op.

Then, back at Desert One all hell broke loose. A bus full of Iranian travelers lumbered down a nearby road and was detained by US troops, which meant witnesses. Another helicopter, moving on the ground to refuel, collided with one of the MC-130s and both aircraft exploded and burned. Eight Americans were killed. Colonels Kyle and Beckwith decided to abandon the rest of the choppers rather than try to fly them out, and to leave in the C-130s. That withdrawal proved successful, but Eagle Claw had been a failure.

What Was the Holloway Report?

The Joint Chiefs of Staff commissioned a postmortem study of the things that had gone wrong with Eagle Claw, known by the name of the study group's chairman, Admiral James L. Holloway III. The members included General Leroy Manor, leader of the Sontay raid; an army helicopter expert, an air force special ops veteran, an army intelligence maven, and a senior marine. Their three-month inquiry reached conclusions both on the specifics of the mission and of a broader nature. The group found that the rescue mission had indeed been feasible, and that it had launched at a practicable time after attaining the necessary readiness posture. There had been adequate resources. A larger number of backup helicopters might have made a difference but would also have affected feasibility and operational security. Eagle Claw, the Holloway group agreed, had been a high-risk mission from the start and was absolutely dependent upon the secrecy with which it was conducted. Once the Iranian bus happened along—a random event—mission security was inevitably compromised.

In a number of ways, because of its more general conclusions, the Holloway Report became fundamental to the evolution of special operations forces. For one thing the study group found that while command control had been excellent at the highest level—the White House, the Joint Chiefs, and General Vaught—it became more tenuous further down the command chain. In good part this was because Eagle Claw was carried out by a scratch team, experts all, but men from different armed services, tapped for the mission, and thrown together with only incidental familiarity with each other. The joint task force had had to begin by inventing itself, setting up a staff, constructing the plan, selecting the units, and training the force. Similar problems applied to the operating units: Delta Force troopers had not worked with the air force planes that took them to Desert One, marine pilots were flying navy helicopters, and so forth. Further, the urgency of the rescue and the need for secrecy had prevented General Vaught's force from conducting a full-scale end-to-end rehearsal of the mission. The thrust of the Holloway Report's general conclusion thus encouraged creation of a permanent "joint task force" structure that could provide a framework around which a tailored operation could quickly coalesce. This concept would result in the creation of the US Special Operations Command. An evolution toward that began at the end of 1980, when the Joint Special Operations Command was set up at Pope Air Force Base.

What Else Changed?

The failure of Operation Eagle Claw led to the formation of new kinds of Special Forces units. One sprang from Robert Meadows's clandestine infiltration of Tehran. It was apparent as soon as the smoke cleared from the US helicopters left burning in the Iranian desert that the hostage rescue had failed during the first phase of the mission, and that the actual rescue would have depended upon the success of the infiltrators' arrangements in Tehran itself. Delta Force had had some trouble with the CIA in preparing the Meadows expedition, and the agency itself had lacked networks suitable to support a military operation. As with the particular, so with the more general: given its focus on intelligence, the CIA had few officers with the particular skills required to pave the way for a Special Forces operation.

Military leaders considered it preferable to forge a permanent capacity to "prepare the battlefield," in its jargon—to do the things, on the ground, in the target area, that would be essential to the success of a special operation. It would be like having a Dick Meadows plus a cohort of similarly dedicated operators available when they were needed. The military already possessed bits and pieces of this. For example, the navy had "Task Force 157," effectively a clan of spies assigned to watch ports. And defense attachés in US embassies could be pressed into service for clandestine purposes—for example, an attaché in Santiago, Chile, had run guns and money to Chilean military officers in 1970, when Washington had wanted to prevent Chilean president-elect Salvador Allende from assuming power. In 1979, when dictator Anastasio Somoza's power crumbled under pressure from the Nicaraguan revolution, a threat had emerged to another US embassy. President Carter had no taste for a repeat of the Iranian embassy takeover. Special Forces infiltrated troopers under civilian cover to bolster the embassy's protection. But there existed nothing like a dedicated unit for clandestine work.

With the Iran hostage crisis still playing out, President Carter considered a second, more robust, rescue mission. Dick Meadows, it was clear, could not be used again. The new unit first formed to take up his mantle. The army set up the Field Operations Group (FOG) under Colonel Jerry King, who had been chief of staff of the joint task force for Eagle Claw, a few months after the Desert One failure. FOG operatives scoured Iran for data on where the militants had moved the hostages, but the repeat mission never took place—the Iranians responded to negotiators instead, releasing the hostages on the day Ronald Reagan took office.

In 1981 Colonel King presided as FOG transmogrified into the Intelligence Support Activity (ISA). It has since existed under this and other names. The ISA had roles in the series of recurrent crises in Beirut in the 1980s, culminating in truck bombings of a US Marine barracks and of the American embassy; in the CIA effort to sustain Nicaraguan Contra rebels attempting to overthrow their government, and in a number of terrorist incidents or operations. These shadow warriors also contributed to the surveillance of Ilich Ramirez Sanchez ("Carlos the Jackal"), who had carried out terror attacks across Europe. He would be apprehended in the Sudan in 1994. Support Activity operatives have also been active in the Bosnian civil war of the 1990s and more recent conflicts. As seems to happen with distressing frequency, the existence of this top-secret unit would be revealed through controversy. In ISA's case this came in 1982 when former Green Beret Major James G. ("Bo") Gritz conducted a freelance foray into Laos, to verify reports that American prisoners left behind from the Vietnam War were still held there. It emerged that the Gritz expedition had preempted an actual US government mission—in which ISA would have participated—with the same goal, and also that Gritz had been given ISA money and carried its equipment and intel.

Another development that resulted from the Desert One failure would be creation of a helicopter unit dedicated to Special Forces missions. A weakness of the hostage rescue force had been that pilots had to be recruited for the operation, and married to choppers that were not their own. Aviation specialists with the 101st Airborne Division, which contained a number of the army's best chopper pilots, were assigned late in 1980 to create a formation melding expert crews with the necessary mix of helicopters to carry out clandestine assignments. The men began training in night flying and the army initiated development of night vision goggles—another Special Forces innovation now used widely far beyond their realm—to facilitate low-visibility activities. The unit, initially known as Task Force 160, acquired the nickname "Nightstalkers." A decade later the Nightstalkers were renamed the 160th Special Operations Aviation Regiment (Airborne), bearing the banner under which they fly today.

With the creation of a sort of private air force, and what amounted to their own spy organization, Special Operations Forces had regenerated the full spectrum of capabilities that had existed in Vietnam in the Studies and Observation Group. In the Joint Special Operations Command the secret warriors also now had a planning element permanently prepared for large-scale covert missions. Unconventional warfare was poised to leap into a new future.

4

TOWARD NEW HORIZONS

ABSTRACT

Special Operations Forces would benefit from the Reagan defense buildup, but they entered the 1980s still suffering the effects of the post-Vietnam emphasis on conventional warfighting. The US invasion of Grenada in 1983 involved Special Forces in many crucial capacities and revealed serious weaknesses in SOF capabilities. This resulted in more focused attention from the Reagan administration, which created a program specifically to improve the forces. But the key development would be passage of the Goldwater-Nichols Act in 1986, which created the US Special Operations Command, for the first time putting SOF from all the armed services under the same top leadership. Not long afterward SOF provided broad demonstrations of their abilities in the 1989 intervention in Panama and the 1990–91 Persian Gulf war. As the United States moved toward increased involvement in peacetime operations and "peacemaking" activities, the SOF acquired new missions in humanitarian interventions, narcoterrorism, counterterrorism, and other roles. While tactics and methods did not change so much, the goals were different, and the new operations placed a greater emphasis on psychological warfare and civil affairs activities. As a battle of Mogadishu showed in 1993, things did not always go well. Nevertheless SOF were busy through the Clinton administration in a broad range of actions in Europe, the Americas, and Africa. Nevertheless the growing importance of SOF

*within the US military has yet to result in any significant represen-
tation of Special Operations Forces officers among the top ranks of
American military commanders.*

As Special Operations Forces moved into the 1980s, they
had a new sense of commitment, within a US defense policy
offering favorable portents. Toward the end of his administration, President Carter had begun to create a "rapid deployment force" capable of short-notice deployment to meet crises
around the globe. With their regional expertise, constant overseas training missions, and small-unit mobility Special Forces
fit that framework very nicely. They were also favored by
American political trends. Ronald Reagan won the presidency
in the 1980 election and came to office promising to re-energize
US military programs.

The Reagan administration feared Soviet military power.
Besides their claims about Russian ballistic missiles and
Moscow's blue water navy, officials made a great deal out
of *Soviet* Special Forces, which Moscow called *spetsnaz*. But
while the administration readily resorted to unfavorable com-
parisons between American and Russian Special Forces, and
added billions of dollars to US military spending, it was slower
to demonstrate its commitment and create specific programs
to increase Special Operations Forces. The most significant
early development was the late 1982 establishment of the First
Special Operations Command (SOCOM), an umbrella headquarters for all Army Special Forces. Yet most of the new units
and capabilities had been set up under Jimmy Carter. Over
the first several years of the Reagan administration the actual
number of Green Berets grew by fewer than a thousand.

What Happened in Grenada?

The US invasion of Grenada in October 1983 served as a
wake-up call for defense planners and the Reagan administration. Critiquing the rationale for this intervention, Operation

Urgent Fury, can await another writing. But the execution of Urgent Fury, like the Iranian hostage rescue, revealed glaring weaknesses in US capabilities. Granted, the invasion was organized on the fly, in a matter of just days after a coup d'état on that Caribbean island seemed to threaten the lives of American residents there. Urgent Fury posed the first serious test of the rapid deployment force.

The major components in the intervention were marines of an amphibious unit on its way to the Mediterranean and paratroopers of the Eighty-Second Airborne Division, but in important ways Urgent Fury can be viewed as a Special Operations Forces battle. SEALs of Team Four were the first US troops on the island, preparing the way for the marine landing, while SEAL Team Six, a new organization created to parallel the Army's Delta Force, was slated to scout the Point Salines airfield. Some of the air force's special tactics troopers would come in with them. Rangers of the army's Seventy Fifth Regiment would do the fighting at Point Salines. Delta Force was to land and secure the Americans held captive. More than two thousand special operations troops participated in all, a quarter of the entire US force. They were assigned to take seven of the eight first-day objectives.

Pretty much everything imaginable went wrong. The airlift was hampered in that the senior commander of the transports happened to be away, and higher officers, on secrecy grounds, prevented his deputy from bringing in top planners until just forty-eight hours before the operation. Communications were a nightmare. There was just a single secure telephone at Military Airlift Command headquarters. The bulk of important calls had to be made from anonymous off-base public telephones. Officers scrambled around looking for quarters to feed the phones.

The Joint Special Operations Command (JSOC) troops were to be committed a day ahead of the main US force. No advance reconnaissance by scouts of the Intelligence Security Activity took place because JSOC distrusted its performance. And the

Command got just nine hours to cobble together its end of the operation. The secrecy meant that messages regarding Urgent Fury were so closely held that key actors were unaware of it. Maps of Grenada were poor. The brass repeatedly changed the missions assigned to the forces.

Water landing of the SEAL Team Six commandos at dusk had to be delayed until the middle of the night and then went awry amid high winds and time differences. Captain Robert A. Gormly, who had led the unit for only three months, did not know that Team Six had never performed a night boat drop, or one by swimmers. One platoon lost nearly half its operators, who drowned in the sea, and the others were unable to find the assault boat supposed to carry them to shore, which had capsized on the airdrop. They had to be rescued. The other platoon got into the water okay and made their rendezvous with the boat but had to postpone further action when it began to take on water. Gormly had another boat parachuted to the SEALs, waiting aboard a destroyer, the next day, which turned out to be a good thing. That night their original boat also capsized, and they had motor problems with the new one. The SEALs and air force forward controllers finally returned to their base ship.

SEAL commander Gormly himself went in on a chopper with another party that aimed to capture the governor general's house, where he would set up his command post. His helo, one of nine Nightstalker birds, was badly damaged and barely made it back to the US flagship. The SEALs who did land were left without their satellite phone when the choppers were driven away by the gunfire. At Point Salines the Rangers parachuted from very low altitude to reduce their vulnerability. They too came under fire. Their quick insertion to secure the airfield turned into a battle with Cuban combat engineers who had been working on the airfield. The Cubans were expecting the assault and put up a fierce fight but had little chance against the heavily supported American troops. But the clumsiness of the air drop stuck in the craw.

Nightstalkers of Task Force 160 had their own problems. Delay of the marines' beach landing meant they had to fly in daylight. Their door guns had been loaded with the wrong type of ammunition. The biggest airmobile assault of the operation would be putting B Squadron of Delta Force atop Richmond Hill prison. Intense flak flamed one helicopter and hit others. On one ship half the men were wounded. Finally, hovering above the prison, they could see it had been completely abandoned. Shades of the Sontay raid! (Though, in this case, the problem was not so much flawed intel as the haste with which the invasion had been thrown together.) The remaining Nightstalkers made for the navy ships offshore. Of the nineteen Americans who died in Urgent Fury, nine were from the Special Operations Forces. Most of the hundred wounded were too. But the island was secured within a matter of a few days.

What Did Ronald Reagan Do?

The Grenada invasion accomplished its goals, but it also revealed a host of weaknesses among the Special Operations Forces. Two 1985 incidents demonstrated other sorts of problems. That June Lebanese terrorists hijacked an American airliner, TWA Flight 847, which they made fly to Beirut, then Algiers, then Beirut again. In Beirut they murdered a US Navy diver, Richard Stethem. A unit of SEAL Team Six plus some air force special tactics experts, elements of the Joint Special Operations Task Force under Brigadier General Carl W. Stiner, were sent to Sicily, then Cyprus, to attempt a hostage rescue of the TWA passengers. But they had to play a catch-up game with the terrorists flitting from place to place, further hindered by air force red tape, which kept its large transport planes at a different state of alert and prevented them being available at the critical moment.

Six months later, in October, came the *Achille Lauro* affair, in which militants took over an Italian cruise ship while it lay docked in Egypt, then murdered Leon Klinghoffer, a disabled American citizen. Again General Stiner led a unit of SOF troops—SEALs, Nighthawks, air force special tactics people—to the Mediterranean. In a repeat of the earlier incident they bounced between Sicily and Cyprus while events played out at sea. This time the terrorists were apprehended and brought to the Italian airbase at Sigonella, Sicily. Stiner's operators were in the process of returning to the United States when the last of them were diverted to follow the plane carrying the terrorists, land behind it, and apprehend them for trial in the United States. But Italy—a NATO ally—had jurisdiction at Sigonella, which was the Italians' airbase after all, and they took a dim view of American troops spiriting away the pirates who had taken over an Italian ship. Their troops surrounded Stiner's operators. The incident came close to a firefight between two allies in which SEALs might have become casualties.

Both affairs demonstrated that diplomatic niceties could bedevil special operations, while the TWA hijacking also held lessons for cooperation between regulars and unconventional forces. President Reagan had already initiated a dedicated buildup of the forces. Secretary of Defense Caspar Weinberger explained this initiative in the defense program he rolled out the previous year. There was a certain hyperbole in Weinberger's Pentagon posture statement, which declared that "over the last three years, we have made significant progress," but he was on the level in saying that "revitalizing our Special Operations Forces (SOF) remains one of this Administration's highest priorities."[1] The interservice issues and political-military misalignments needed to be dealt with separately.

Among the changes introduced in the aftermath of Grenada were the creation of an "agency" under the Joint Chiefs to manage the forces, the creation of a permanent Joint Special Operations Task Force (JSOTF) to carry out missions, and a directive to the Joint Staff of the JCS to recommend an organizational structure to improve effectiveness. The Reagan administration began upgrading the forces. The army took existing battalions from several groups to reactivate the First Special Forces Group—the biggest strength accretion in several years (and the first Vietnam-era Green Beret unit to return to duty). The Pentagon planned to add another Special Forces Group, another SEAL team, plus a psychological warfare battalion and more civil affairs experts. Delta Force would add an additional battalion, and another would join the Seventy-Fifth Ranger Regiment. All the SOF were to be at full strength by 1988. For the first time the army created a career track for special operations. At this point the air force became the only armed service *not* to have a military occupational specialty for this activity.

The Reagan SOF buildup featured considerable dependence upon nonactive forces. Armed services Reserve Forces and the National Guard SOF components outnumbered active duty operators in every branch. For the army in 1987 there would be four active Special Forces and an equal number in the Reserve or National Guard. Three-quarters of psychological warfare battalions would be in the Reserve. Naval Reserves included nearly as many SEAL teams, and an equal number of special boat teams as there were on active duty.

The air force had made repeated efforts to get rid of the unconventional warfare mission. One was to move its airlift assets, in the 1970s to the Tactical Air Command, during the Reagan years to the Military Airlift Command. Only one special operations squadron existed in the Air Force Reserve, but the service's practice of concentrating transport formations in the Reserve or Air Guard meant that there were more than four airmen in SOF roles in the reserve forces for every one on active service. Those reserve airmen alone numbered more than all the regular SOF operators in all the armed services combined. In all there were nearly 15,000 regulars, but the total number of Special Operations Forces in 1987 amounted to 48,265.

Despite the renewed emphasis on Special Operations Forces as commando-style raiders (the Pentagon parlance was "direct action"), their role in helping train the military in foreign lands continued. Between 1975 and 1985 more than five hundred mobile training teams were sent to nearly sixty countries. Some of these played a role in CIA covert operations, such as the Green Beret teams who trained the Honduran army, which shielded the CIA's Nicaraguan Contra rebels against cross-border incursions by Sandinista troops. Delta Force also participated in patrols and maneuvers in Honduras.

The parallel civil war in El Salvador involved Green Berets in a way that made their training teams no longer "mobile," except in the sense that teams rotated through the country and replaced each other. This mission endured for more than a decade. In 1981 Berets of the Seventh Group trained the Salvadoran Atlacatl Light Infantry Battalion, and another of these units got its training right at Fort Bragg the following year. The Atlacatl Battalion was responsible later for a notorious massacre of Salvadoran villagers. (Green Beret opinions of that affair remain unknown.)

After 1983 the United States set up a regional center in Honduras that provided training for Salvadorans and troops from other Latin countries. SOF were also assigned directly as advisers to each of the Salvadorans' infantry brigades. In 1987 a Seventh Group trooper, Sergeant First Class Gregory A. Fronius, died in battle when Marxist guerrillas assaulted the headquarters to which he had been assigned. The Central American wars ended early in the first Bush administration with multilateral agreements and political settlements within the countries.

What Innovations Came to SOF?

Innovation in aerial capabilities and in underwater launch for SEALs or other reconnaissance troops were quite notable over the 1980s and into the 1990s. Air Force Special Operations had atrophied after Vietnam, and Desert One had demonstrated that its MC-130E Combat Talons absolutely required a capability to refuel in the air. In Grenada there were difficulties with electronic systems. In between the air force commissioned a "Combat Talon II" (MC-130H), and an aerial tanker version, the MC-130P, that arrived on the flight line in 1986. The Talon II program was critically delayed by program decisions that moved funding elsewhere or provided for inferior avionics suites. The full-version aircraft did not become available until 1991. Then both planes possessed the improved electronics and precision onboard navigation systems necessary for special operations.

Naval developments are perhaps the most interesting. The submarine *Grayback* with its ability to launch combat swimmers from underwater was old and near the end of its service life. Spare parts were gone. She was finally decommissioned in 1984—and actually sunk as a target in a live-fire training exercise off the Philippines. Somewhere along the line planners realized that the preferred solution was not to build a specialized submarine but a "dry deck shelter"—a container that could be attached to a sub that SEALs could enter from inside the boat before filling with water, whereupon the combat swimmers could launch into the sea. These could be installed on a wider range of boats modified to carry them. Design began in the late 1970s. The first of these shelters, built by the General Dynamics Corporation, was completed in 1982. Under Caspar Weinberger the Pentagon planned for three shelter-equipped submarines in each of the Atlantic and Pacific Fleets—a much more ample capacity than anything the Naval Special Warfare Command had ever had. The second of these submarine attachments did not materialize until 1987, but thereafter they were delivered annually, until the full set of six was available in 1991. Later, when nuclear arms reduction agreements resulted in the disarming of some of the large *Ohio*-class Trident missile submarines, a few of them were converted to troop carriers to work with the dry shelters. This represented a considerable capability increase.

Both the aircraft and the naval vessels remain active today.

What Is the Special Operations Command?

The US Special Operations Command (USSOCOM) is a strategic command for all US Special Forces. It resulted from the efforts of some key political and military leaders and the hopes of members of the Special Forces community. The Joint Special Operations Agency commanded no troops and had no operational authority. Without an integrated program for familiarizing the troops, training them, designing innovations in tactics, and putting new equipment into the pipeline, the agency did little to increase readiness or capabilities. The Special Operations Command's JSOTF could not require other armed services to undertake supporting actions. Thus, while the Reagan buildup created a longer troop list, no institutional changes matched the force growth. In addition, the armed services, particularly the air force, still had a tendency to repurpose budget funds intended for Special Forces. A more comprehensive mechanism remained necessary.

Initiatives to reframe the US military were already underway in the Congress. There the interest lay principally in reducing waste and duplication, plus the interservice rivalries that resulted from two different chains of command—one from the president through the secretary of defense to the troops, the other from the Joint Chiefs of Staff downward. Arizona Republican Senator Barry Goldwater and Alabama Democrat Representative William F. Nichols sponsored a bill to completely reorganize the military structure. Under the Goldwater-Nichols concept the actual troop commands would take precedence. In US practice there existed "unified commands"—such as the Commander-in-Chief (C-in-C) Pacific—who exercised control over all forces of all armed services in their regional or functional arena. The new idea was to have the chain of command run from the president through the chairman (and vice chairman) of the Joint Chiefs direct to the C-in-Cs. The defense secretary would assist the president in his decisions and manage the armed services through their civilian leadership, with the goal of developing and maintaining the weapons and forces the C-in-Cs required. In October 1986 President Reagan signed the Goldwater-Nichols Act into law.

For our purposes the key question was whether Special Operations Forces should have their own C-in-C. Led by Admiral William J. Crowe, many regulars in the services opposed this. One key moment on Capitol Hill came when Major General Richard A. Scholtes of the army, who had led JSOC in the Grenada invasion, testified as to how conventional force commanders had misused Special Forces during the operation. Not only did the SOF win their argument, they got more. Under an amendment proposed by Senators Sam Nunn (D-GA) and William Cohen (R-ME) a new era would begin. There would be a C-in-C, a four-star general officer over USSOCOM, there would be a special budget line for SOF fenced off from poaching, and at the level of the secretary of defense a new assistant secretary position would be created specifically to deal with Special Forces and low-intensity conflict. Each of the regional C-in-Cs would have a component command for all Special Forces operating in its area. This was written into Goldwater-Nichols. The command came into being in April 1987 under army general James J. Lindsay.

Was There Resentment within the Military When SOF Got Their Own Command?

The short answer is yes. Secretary Weinberger held back the military's psychological warfare and civil affairs units pending a further review. He delayed the appointment of the new assistant secretary, who was supposed to oversee these activities at the Pentagon. The Joint Chiefs' delineation of USSOCOM missions focused on preparation of the forces and largely left out the conduct of operations except where directed by the president and secretary of defense. Admiral

Crowe spoke of the need for the silent warriors to educate the rest of the military on their nature and capabilities. This represented a virtual reversal of the Kennedy administration posture, which had been that in the future the best soldier would be the man or woman who understood special operations and could employ them alongside conventional ones. Rather than the armed services inculcating everyone with a sensitivity for unconventional warfare, now the onus was (again) on the special operators to convince others of their utility.

By far the most contentious issue would be the relationships between and among the C-in-Cs. The USSOCOM could build and arm its forces and plan their missions, but the operations would be carried out in geographic areas that were the responsibility of the regional C-in-Cs. The affinity between the C-in-Cs and the special operations component commanders within their regions depended entirely upon the supremos' attitudes toward unconventional warfare. Obtaining the confidence of the regional commands and their cooperation with SOF needs proved to be a continuing headache, still not fully resolved when the 9/11 attacks triggered the war on terror. The difficulties between the special operators and CENTCOM at the battle of Tora Bora, related at the outset of this narrative, owed something to this continuing resentment. As it happened, both the USSOCOM and CENTCOM had their main headquarters in Florida, at MacDill Air Force Base in Tampa, so there had to be plentiful opportunities for cross-pollination. Vestigial resentment of Special Forces proved hard to shake.

What Happened in the Persian Gulf?

Almost immediately the Special Operations Forces got a fresh opportunity to demonstrate their worth. A war between Iran and Iraq had begun in 1980 and continued still. By 1986 this had come to include the sides conducting economic warfare against each other by attacking oil tankers in the Persian Gulf, reducing the adversaries' national income but also threatening world oil supplies. The Reagan administration responded by reflagging some Kuwaiti tankers under the American flag, but this was insufficient in the face of the Iranians' major weapon, the naval mine. Tehran could argue that it was protecting coastal waters, not specifically attacking the tankers falling victim to these mines. Something needed to be done to obstruct the Iranian minelaying itself. The CENTCOM, then under General George B. Crist, planned Operation Earnest Will to counter the Iranians. By the summer of 1987 it had become clear that SOF had the best capabilities to cope with the minelaying, which took place at night. The army's Nightstalkers and the Naval Special Warfare Command's fast patrol boats, SEAL platoons, and Special Boat Units were called out to counter the Iranians. The choppers helped escort convoys and attacked Iranian minelaying vessels. SEALs boarding one of these ships obtained evidence the Iranians were deliberately placing mines in international waters. SEALs also helped destroy Iranian offshore oil rigs in retaliation for a cruise missile attack against one of the reflagged oil tankers, and again following the mining of the US frigate *Samuel B. Roberts* in 1988. The last SOF returned home that summer, after Iranian attacks had diminished and the war was about to end with a United Nations–brokered ceasefire. While much is said today about American troops serving three, four, or more tours in the Iraq and Afghan wars, in this Persian Gulf fight some of the USSOCOM operators did two or three rotations in the Gulf, and with a lot less down time in between assignments.

What Happened in Panama?

The Reagan administration gave way to the presidency of George H. W. Bush. A little over a year after the Persian Gulf mission, President Bush intervened in Panama against the regime of military strongman Manuel Noriega. First there was a show of force, Operation Nimrod Dancer, in connection with a failed coup attempt against Noriega. Operators from Delta Force and SEAL Team Six were among the American troops deployed to the Canal Zone. A few months later came Operation Just Cause, where the SOF contribution would be critical. With the evolution of the C-in-C command structure, Just Cause also featured the first use of a Joint Special Operations Task Force in the SOUTHCOM region, the C-in-C for Latin America. Major General Wayne A. Downing, who had been a squadron leader with Delta Force at Desert One, and now headed the Joint Special Operations Command, personally led the JSOTF for Just Cause. It was the most complex mission yet attempted by the unconventional warfare forces—this time not merely the tip of the spear but a major slice of the entire US complement. To the surprise of everyone but Downing and his operators, their parts of the intervention, though not without a hitch, came off splendidly.

Downing set up three separate forces for different missions. Small groups of direct action troops had ancillary tasks. The largest element by far relied on detachments of Rangers to make airborne assaults on the main base of the Panamanian air force (and the country's major international airport) plus another key airport at Rio Hato. Air force special tactics troopers went in ahead to place navigation beacons. The Rangers needed to strike the air force base/airport with blitzkrieg timing because paratroops were slated to come in just forty-five minutes after them. They cleared enough of the field to accomplish that goal, secured most of their objectives within two hours, and took the surrender of the last Panamanian defense forces four hours into the mission. At Rio Hato Panamanian defenders' antiaircraft fire struck many of the transport aircraft, but the airdrop still succeeded. Other direct action groups hit Modelo Prison, where they freed an American citizen held there; secured both sides of the Panama Canal to preclude sabotage; took the airfield where Noriega kept his personal jet, and captured a key bridge.

The central purpose of Just Cause was the capture of Manual Noriega. A task force that combined Special Forces with regular mechanized troops surrounded and attacked the Commandancia, Noriega's headquarters in Panama City. But the Americans did not know exactly where Noriega was, and the strongman escaped immediate capture. After that Downing's operators went after the Panamanian's known hangouts and associates, hoping to catch the general. Running out of hiding places, after four days Noriega sought refuge at the Papal Nunciature. At that point Special Forces surrounded the compound and psychological warfare specialists began a campaign aimed specifically at him, hoping that blaring music would wear him down. Diplomats negotiated Noriega's surrender and SOF would take him into custody on January 3, 1990. The rest was all details. Special Operations Forces had formed the cutting edge of a major US invasion. Only twenty-three Americans were killed in combat during Just Cause, but nearly half of them were from Wayne Downing's command.

Was Panama the Apex of Special Forces' Work in the First Bush Administration?

No. Actually USSOCOM efforts peaked back in the Persian Gulf, in the most intense extended special operation since Vietnam. The war began that same summer when the Iraqi forces of Saddam Hussein invaded Kuwait. The Bush administration initiated Operation Desert Shield to prevent any Iraqi incursion into Saudi Arabia, and the United States with a coalition of international partners then conducted Operation Desert Storm to drive the Iraqis out of Kuwait. SOF had important roles in Desert Shield / Desert Storm. The CENTCOM Special Operations Command was first on the scene, with troopers arriving at Riyadh on August 10, 1990. The SEALs and air force operators led the way, and two battalions of the Fifth Special Forces Group joined them a couple of weeks later.

General Norman Schwarzkopf, the CENTCOM commander, held back the operators. Early on, Brigadier General Richard Potter Jr., chief of the special operations task force in Europe, had visited Turkey to quietly evaluate the potential for starting an anti-Saddam resistance movement among the Kurds of Iraq's bordering northern marches. A former Delta trooper, Potter liked the idea. Half the Tenth Special Forces Group came to Turkey for the mission, using the cover that they were preparing a rescue network for downed pilots. Schwarzkopf nixed the plan. He wanted nothing to give away his intentions. Meanwhile an SOF-developed intelligence data-handling system helped the American C-in-C make sense of the millions of bits of information constantly flowing into CENTCOM headquarters.

The operators were crucial during Desert Shield in helping to put the Saudi military into fighting shape as well as in reconstituting the Kuwaiti navy and later its army. More than 30,000 soldiers and sailors from Saudi and Kuwait took their lessons from Fifth Special Forces and the SEALs. When the fighting actually started in January 1991, Special Forces accompanied the units, giving advice, calling in air support, and liaising with US commanders. Special operations troops succeeded in rescuing several pilots who had been forced to parachute over enemy territory. Psychological warfare troops worked hard to undermine Iraqi morale. Judging from Iraqi combat performance in that war, they were pretty successful. Psy-war radio broadcasts capitalized on a previous campaign that had dropped millions of "safe conduct" passes over Iraqi troop concentrations. More than 86,000 Iraqi soldiers were taken prisoner during the war, and most of them had the safe-conduct passes.

There were mission-critical forays as well. The Desert Storm phase of the conflict began with an air campaign in which coalition warplanes pounded Iraqi defenses and strategic targets. Before the first wave of aircraft flew into Iraqi territory, Special Forces mounted a direct action to neutralize

Iraqi warning systems, command networks, and air defenses, creating a safe corridor for the coalition warplanes. Air force special tactics troops placed navigation beacons along the Iraqi-Saudi border to guide aircraft through the cleared corridor and the others that followed. A SEAL platoon helped defend the town of Khafji against the only substantial Iraqi ground incursion of the war. The ground offensive launched in late February. Its linchpin would be a wide left pincer attack by an armored corps of American and British troops. A week ahead of time Special Forces operators scouted the ground over which the forces would transit, making sure the tanks and mechanized troops would be able to move through this country. A SEAL mission at the outset of the coalition attack sought to make the Iraqis believe the United States was about to launch an amphibious invasion. Just prior to the offensive more SOF were inserted for long-range reconnaissance purposes, reporting on Iraqi military moves behind the lines.

Most important was the rescue mission code-named "Pacific Wind." During all the months of preparation Iraqis had used the US embassy in Kuwait City to house Americans, Europeans, and others, effectively a band of hostages. SOF planned Pacific Wind to get them out. But Washington doubts and CENTCOM rejections hobbled the preparations, and then a month before the war Saddam Hussein suddenly freed the hostages himself. The SOF plan now transmuted into an op to liberate the embassy building. As the SOF-trained Kuwaiti-Saudi army moved to recapture their capital, a fast attack unit from Third Group sped ahead. Operators prepared a simultaneous air assault, with SOF fast-roping from Nightstalker helicopters hovering above.

All of these efforts would be important to the success of Desert Storm, but what SOF are probably most remembered for is "Scud hunting." Saddam Hussein had a stock of medium-range ballistic missiles, Russian-made rockets called Scuds by their NATO adversaries, that could reach as far as Israel and middle Saudi Arabia. Saddam also had chemical weapons and promised to ignite a conflagration with these WMD. He launched missiles at both Israel and Saudi Arabia. Fortunately the Scuds' accuracy was so poor that almost all these rockets landed far from critical targets, and most of them were armed with conventional explosives. Tactical antimissile systems in Israel and Saudi Arabia also knocked down some of the rockets. Nevertheless, the greatest loss of life among coalition forces in this war came when a Scud hit one of the American rear bases along the Persian Gulf.

Neutralizing the Scud threat became a key coalition objective. A squadron of Delta Force, some British Special Air Service troopers, some of the Nightstalkers, and other coalition air forces were committed to the effort. The Iraqis had some fixed missile bases and these were pounded from the air. But they also had mobile launchers and were good at hiding them, even in the desert. The first cross-border Scud hunt set the pattern. A team of sixteen operators entered Iraq on two vehicles several weeks ahead of the invasion. They hid in the daytime and scouted at night, and when they saw a missile, they called in 160th Aviation's Blackhawk choppers to blast them. One week into the campaign General Schwarzkopf was impressed enough with the results that he added a Ranger company and more Nightstalkers to the effort. SOF were soon running four teams at a time against the Scuds.

Although Desert Storm would be a massive conventional invasion and General Schwarzkopf a skeptic about Special Forces, in the end the SOF proved so useful in so many ways that their role in the conflict was significant. More than 7,700 SOF troopers fought in the war, with another thousand in Turkey for the abortive Kurdish mission. The latter got to enter Iraq after all, almost immediately after the war, to help secure Kurdish territory for a humanitarian mission. Almost 20 percent of the 147 American service members killed in the war were from the Special Operations Forces.

How Has the Changing Nature of US Interventions Impacted the Role of the Special Operations Forces?

There *were* changes in SOF activities as the nature of US interventions altered through the 1990s. This began immediately at the end of Desert Storm. There was concern at that point about the Kurds in northern Iraq, many of whom had fled their homes during the fighting. British and US forces in small numbers furnished a security cordon, behind which SOF civil affairs specialists began a major humanitarian relief operation. This was called "Provide Comfort" and included the establishment of refugee camps, delivery of food and other materials, and assistance in re-establishing the villages.

Provide Comfort became the first of a number of actions that were humanitarian in some form. Seeking a way to analyze these kinds of activity, some observers took to calling them "peacemaking," as opposed to more familiar peacekeeping or straight military actions. Special Forces continued to do many of the same kinds of things—patrolling, securing key objectives by means of direct action, engaging in civic actions, and advising local authorities—but the purposes of SOF activity changed. Through the 1990s US humanitarian interventions took place in Somalia (1992–95), Bosnia-Herzegovina (1995 onwards), Kosovo (1999) and Haiti (1994–95). Special Forces engineer specialists also engaged in a mine-clearing program in Cambodia and instructed foreign nationals—for example Afghans—how to teach these skills to others and help clear mines from their own conflict zones.

Of all the peacemaking operations, "Restore Hope" and its successors in Somalia was the one that led to the most painful SOF experience. This came in the battle of Mogadishu. It all began with the SEALs, who landed ahead of a force of US Marines plus army troops of the Tenth Mountain Division. President George H. W. Bush sent them in to secure the land in December 1992. Somalia had become a humanitarian disaster area amid the depredations of warring clans. Units of SEAL Team Two, the Fifth Special Forces Group, psychological warfare experts, and civil affairs officers participated. The mission was initially successful, and humanitarian aid began to flow again. Only about a month later the Bush administration gave way to the presidency of William J. Clinton. It would be Bill Clinton who presided over the painful part of the operation.

In the spring of 1993 the American force in Somalia packed its bags and gave way to a United Nations operation. Not long afterward the restive clans renewed their fight, this time targeting the UN troops. President Clinton called on Air Force SOF to deploy AC-130 gunships to fly support missions for embattled UN forces. When that proved insufficient, he ordered the deployment of a Joint Special Operations Task Force that consisted primarily of Rangers and Nightstalkers but also included operators from SEAL Team Six, C Squadron of the Delta Force, and air force special tactics personnel. Specialists of the Intelligence Support Activity ran Somali agents among the clans. In all there were about 450 SOF troopers. A key target for the Americans, called Task Force Ranger, was the warlord Mohamed Farah Aideed. Between August and October 1993 Task Force Ranger launched seven attempts to capture Aideed.

The seventh raid went awry. It has been memorialized in the book and movie *Blackhawk Down*. The intel was that two of Aideed's key aides would be meeting in a house near Mogadishu's central market. Some hoped the warlord himself might show up. In any case, intelligence was aware the area had become an Aideed stronghold. The plan was for Delta Force operators to assault from Nightstalker ships and take the compound, with a force of Rangers and some SEALs who would insert partly by air and partly by motor vehicle to provide security for the withdrawal. The motorized element would take out the prisoners. A quick reaction force of American infantry was available if needed. Controlling the whole mission from a helicopter was Delta Force squadron commander Lieutenant Colonel Gary Harrell.

The raid went down on October 3. Things went south very fast. The road convoy encountered ambushes on its way to the target area. It was delayed. Even though the Delta strike on the house succeeded, clan resistance intensified quickly. The convoy managed to extract Somali prisoners through another ambush, but was then sent back as part of a scratch reaction force. The reaction force was itself pinned down in heavy fighting and became lost in the tight streets of the city. Several of the prisoners were killed, half the American troops were dead or wounded, and most of the vehicles had been shot up.

One of the 160th Regiment's choppers had come in farther from the objective because of debris on the landing zone. Another was targeted on the ground by grenades. Those got away, but a third of the Blackhawks, hit by a rocket-propelled grenade, crashed. Troopers dashed to rescue the crew while Somalis came at them from another direction. A rescue chopper bringing medics was hit next and had to fight to stay airborne long enough to get back. The medics barely made it to the ground. After that the situation went from bad to worse. Delta operators and Rangers were simultaneously attempting to recover their comrades and casualties and establish a perimeter to hold out, with diminishing ammunition and a swelling enemy. Colonel Harrell managed to get some more operators in to reinforce his beleaguered troops, so eventually about a hundred Americans were fighting desperately to hold a perimeter around the crashed Blackhawk. In epic style they began calling their patch of earth "The Alamo." An attack helicopter supporting them was itself shot down.

The quick reaction force from the Tenth Mountain Division was dispatched to the second helicopter crash site. It was ambushed well short of that place and never made it. They were finally ordered to withdraw, and it took another hour to disentangle themselves. Finally a much heavier force of United Nations troops, with Pakistani tanks, Pakistani and Malaysian infantry, and more American troops, moved off in the night to reach the men at The Alamo. They succeeded, after more adventures as well as trouble with their UN allies, who at a certain point refused to go any farther. When The Alamo was relieved, the Rangers and Delta troopers there had been fighting for ten hours. It took another four to get the raiders to safety. The second crash site was never reached, and Somali militants made a show of the body of one of the Americans killed there. The SOF had suffered eighteen dead, eighty-five wounded, and one prisoner from the second chopper. Warlord Aideed eventually released that soldier. The battle of Mogadishu was a victory but a pyrrhic one. SOF brought back their prisoners, but the bitter fight and losses convinced Washington that heavier forces than the unconventional warriors were necessary. Moreover, why incur such losses for a humanitarian intervention? More Green Berets and SEALs deployed to Somalia briefly, but Task Force Ranger pulled out, and most of the new Americans were tankers or mechanized troops. The Clinton administration withdrew all those US forces from Somalia within less than half a year.

What Other Missions Did Special Forces Conduct?

Clinton's years saw Special Operations Forces in several new humanitarian engagements, in peacemaking and peacekeeping, in their traditional training roles and in counterdrug activities. In Haiti USSOCOM light patrol craft tried to enforce an embargo on weapons shipments into the country and drug transits encouraged by the military regime. When a full-scale intervention came in the fall of 1994, SEALs did the beach reconnaissance, as they had in Somalia. Direct action missions by the Third Special Forces Group then helped calm the political turmoil, securing the countryside while US infantry focused on the capital, Port-au-Prince, ejecting Haitian troops who had overthrown the elected president. Civil affairs teams helped re-energize the Haitian government when the former president returned. The US force handed the mission over to a United Nations contingent that prepared new elections in 1995.

Haitian involvement overlapped with SOF activity in the Balkans. The unconventional warfare component of the US European Command first called on SOF for maritime patrol and surveillance. Once the states of the former Yugoslavia signed peace agreements in late 1995 a NATO Implementation Force was created in Bosnia-Herzegovina and Croatia. This included Americans, among them troopers of the Tenth Special Forces Group, who became vital intermediaries among the multinational array of NATO units and the local authorities. They were also important in the search for aircraft wreckage when a US plane carrying a senior delegation that included Secretary of Commerce Ron Brown crashed outside Dubrovnik in 1996. Civil affairs and psychological warfare units were again crucial. Special Operations Forces helped establish several demining training centers. The mission of separating the warring ethnic groups and demobilizing their forces has continued under several guises since. In 1999, when Kosovo rebelled to secede from Serbia, civil affairs and psychological warfare units had the main role. Special Forces blocked the border to prevent the fighting spilling over into the other Balkan states and conducted patrols inside Kosovo, and an SOF direct action mission destroyed a rail line to inhibit Serb troop movements, while others rescued the only two American pilots shot down during the NATO air campaign against Serbia that formed part of this conflict. In a July 1999 firefight, Captain Robert Schaefer's ODA-056, assigned to liaison with a Russian unit, called in artillery fire to support it, marking the first American military action to succor Russians since before the Cold War.

A noteworthy development arising from all these assorted operations was the important emphasis given to psychological warfare and civil affairs activities, elevating the status of operators in these areas, which have tended to be the poor sisters among Special Forces. This has not, however, led to any significant increase or restructuring of the SOF elements that are dedicated to these missions.

Other events repeatedly drew the shadow warriors to Africa. In 1992 the Special Operations Forces provided the ground security and air elements for an evacuation of American citizens from Sierra Leone, and five years later Green Berets who were in the country on a training mission covered the landing of marines for a second emergency departure. In 1996 SOF reinforced the American embassy in Liberia and assisted in yet another evacuation. The Rwandan genocide of 1994 led to more attention from Washington. Two years later the Third Special Forces Group was tapped as a central element in a new effort to train African national armies so they could undertake peacekeeping missions on the continent. Troops from eight African lands received this training during the Clinton era. USSOCOM also returned to Liberia in greater force during 1998 when there was a direct threat against the US embassy. The SOF helped marines guard the embassy, while a SEAL detachment from Naval Special Warfare Group Two and a couple of SOCOM's light patrol craft maintained a visible presence in the harbor of Monrovia.

In Latin America the major efforts of Special Operations Forces were in interdiction of drug smuggling. Colombian cartel boss Pablo Escobar became the focus of a major manhunt after his 1992 escape from prison. In a project called "Pokeweed," troopers of the Intelligence Support Activity, Delta plus SEAL Team Six trained and advised a Colombian special unit called the Search Bloc. Men of the Intelligence Support Activity and the Colombian Search Bloc cornered Escobar in December 1993. He was killed in a shootout. Colombia continued to descend into the sort of conflict that has come to be called "narcoterrorism." Peru was also a major center, Bolivia a growing region, Mexico and Central America transit centers, and so on. Naval Special Warfare sent some of its light patrol craft to interdict seaborne shipments in the Gulf of Mexico and along the Pacific coastal plain. While the CIA took the lead in Peru, the SOF modified its mobile training teams to instruct local counterdrug units, or assist police forces in many of these countries. The missions involved both Green Berets and SEALs. There was an even greater degree of involvement in Colombia, where US officials were instrumental in devising an integrated strategy called "Plan Colombia." When Bill Clinton entered office in 1992, there were more than a hundred of these SOF counterdrug deployments underway. President Clinton, however, demanded even more action. The military doubled its level of effort.

Are Special Forces Suitable in All Types of Warfare?

The short answer is maybe. This brief narrative demonstrates that Special Operations Forces have played a significant role in a wide variety of types of conflict. There remains the case of major wars. In big wars too, however, SOF have provided strategic reconnaissance, more localized scouting, preparation of the battlefield, a capacity for commando-style action, and training of allied forces. Desert Storm illustrates this nicely. But conventionally trained officers continue to maintain that Special Operations Forces do not provide the combat capability for major hostilities. Again Desert Storm serves to illustrate: General Norman Schwarzkopf remained leery of the SOF right into the war. In one respect the regular troops are right: Special Forces cannot replace conventional forces if the object is mass action. There are simply not enough SOF operators. We will return to this in chapter 6. Another issue is claims from outsiders that turn Special Forces nature and training on their heads to argue SOF do not understand *conventional* warfare. This is not credible in my view. Not only are SOF intimately involved in the training of armed forces in many lands for conventional military missions, but the argument relies partly on the very same military disdain that has retarded the promotion to high rank of SOF officers. Not only have many SOF people shuttled back and forth between conventional and unconventional warfare units, once the operators began to earn their stars, the hierarchy of military commands inevitably put SOF officers into positions that gave them broad exposure to military problems.

What Is the Relationship between Special Forces and the CIA?

This narrative has been replete with examples that suggest a close relationship between Special Operations Forces and the Central Intelligence Agency. In the early days and in Vietnam the CIA provided funding mechanisms and quiet procurement for unusual equipment Special Forces needed. In case after case, intelligence the CIA and other agencies provided was crucial to SOF missions. The Sontay and Iran hostage raids are especially good examples of the CIA's importance to special operations. The SOF have their own intelligence experts, of course, and the operators have often viewed the agency as working at cross-purposes with them. That was one reason for the creation of the Intelligence Support Activity as an SOF entity. Nevertheless, cooperation has remained close. During the 1990s, starting with the Gulf War, there was considerable agitation among the armed services for better, even more integrated support. So-called national assets—the CIA-run programs, and the spy satellites and strategic electronic means run by defense agencies for top-level purposes—it was argued, should be more adaptable to strictly military needs. The CIA even developed the acronym "SMO" (Support for Military Operations) to cover this issue. It was prominent during the US peace operations in the former Yugoslavia as well as the war in Kosovo. Since 9/11 the CIA has been pulled in different directions, with two open wars in progress as well as its own back-alley counterterror fight, but one particular aspect—the drone war, which is discussed below—has thrown SOF and the agency into the same basket.

The relationship is symbiotic. Not only do Special Forces get much from the CIA, they give a fair amount too. Several early CIA clandestine operations chiefs, or chiefs of key geographic regions, were unconventional warfare officers detached from army duty. General Yarborough, who got Special Forces their Green Berets, had been with CIA's predecessor agency in Austria after the end of World War II. CIA's chief of operations for the China coast in the early 1950s had been with Merrill's Marauders. Service in SOF is a major avenue for recruits to the CIA's paramilitary operations division. In Vietnam days most of its case officers with Lao and Cambodian irregulars were former Green Berets. This trend continues. In the late 1990s General Wayne Downing, Iran hostage rescue veteran and once leader of the fabled Special Forces Operational Detachment-Delta, went to the CIA as the number three man in its Operations Directorate.

Have SOF Officers Ever Headed the US Military?

Here the short answer is yes, but not many. Some of the armed services' continuing discomfort with Special Operations Forces may be attributable simply to the evolution of the military machine. With some of the services lacking an SOF career track right through the 1980s, and others only establishing that kind of occupational specialty around then, it's possible that the military just has not had enough time to develop senior officers from SOF's ranks. A look at the very top ranks of the US armed forces shows the dimension of the problem. Since the Goldwater-Nichols Act created the US Special Operations Command forty-nine men (there has yet to be a woman in any of these senior positions) have held the posts of chief of staff of the US Army or Air Force, chief of naval operations, commandant of the Marine Corps, or vice chairman and chairman of the Joint Chiefs of Staff (JCS). Among all these individuals only two had any SOF background. General Hugh Shelton, who served as JCS chairman at the time of 9/11, had been in the Fifth Special Forces Group in Vietnam. General Peter J. Schoomaker, the army's chief of staff from 2003 until 2007, was a real operator, having twice led squadrons of the Delta Force in the 1980s and the full Delta Force from 1989 to 1992.

A few of the others in addition to these two had some direct experience that afforded them knowledge of SOF capabilities. General Dennis J. Reimer, who led the army during Clinton's final years, had had Ranger and airborne training and at least could rub elbows with the Green Berets at Fort Bragg. His contemporary as JCS chairman, General John Shalikashvili, had commanded Operation Provide Comfort in northern Iraq after the Gulf War, where Special Forces civil affairs had the key role. Finally, Admiral David E. Jeremiah, the JCS vice chairman during the Gulf War and after, had led the Mediterranean forces that responded to the *Achille Lauro* pirate incident, where, again, SOF played the major part.

Outsiders can hardly interpret the tea leaves of military personnel choices—or presidents' decisions in selecting these senior leaders—but the record suggests that the military's top leadership has not, heretofore, been especially sympathetic toward Special Operations Forces. "Barbwire Bob" Kingston, who rose from private to full general and was the first head of CENTCOM, was the early exception. General Stanley McChrystal, once a candidate for high office, had his career smashed when a journalist published very negative remarks about President Barack Obama from officers on McChrystal's staff when he commanded in Afghanistan. The future of Admiral William H. McRaven has been instructive. After the takedown of Osama bin Laden, McRaven led USSOCOM. He was a potential candidate for chief of naval operations or even one of the top JCS jobs. Instead, in the summer of 2014 Admiral McRaven retired from the navy to become president of the University of Texas. If Mr. Obama could not select McRaven—reputedly a favorite—for high office, that indicates a continuing distaste among the conventional military for those who have risen through SOF ranks. In the meantime, the September 11 attacks ushered in a new era in which Special Operations Forces became more important than ever.

5

AFTER SEPTEMBER 11

ABSTRACT

The conflict that began with the September 11, 2001, terrorist attacks on the United States ushered in a new period for Special Operations Forces, indeed possibly their most active involvement ever, the Vietnam War included. SOF provided the tip of the spear in two wars—Afghanistan and Iraq—in a range of direct action missions, in an intense psychological warfare campaign, and in active support of CIA operations. The SOF also acquired new roles, as with the operation of drones in an air campaign, while continuing their traditional missions. New SOF problems have developed as well, including relationships with private military contractors, many of whom are former SOF; as well as public disquiet at such SOF activities as the drone war or the night raids so prevalent in Iraq and Afghanistan.

Brigadier General Stanley McChrystal stood near the door of a C-130J transport, ready for a practice parachute jump near Fort Bragg, when the air force jumpmaster leaned over to say something to the lead man, McChrystal's boss. It was September 11, 2001. McChrystal overheard the airman say that a plane had crashed into one of the World Trade Center towers in New York City. The paratroopers jumped. As he floated down to earth McChrystal had scant moments to reflect upon the fresh demands sure to follow this horrific attack. At the moment he was the chief of staff of the Eighteenth Airborne Corps. He and his boss, Lieutenant General Daniel McNeill, the corps commander, led the nation's premier reserve military force. The Eighteenth Airborne Corps, in whole or in part, had been called out for nearly every major US military intervention. The Dominican Republic, Vietnam, Panama, Grenada, the Gulf War—the airborne had seen them all. McNeill's formation typically kept at least one parachute brigade ready to move at all times, with the capability of deploying the remainder of the force over a short time. This time too there were frantic preparations, rumors, wild claims of al-Qaeda anthrax attacks, and more.

But nothing happened. Nothing at all. At least not right away. Instead all the excitement was across Fort Bragg at the special operations compound on Smoke Bomb Hill. A-Teams of Green Berets went to Afghanistan to help newfound Afghan allies. The Rangers deployed to seize those first sites for in-country airbases (see the prologue). It was SOF at the tip of the spear, the new American way of war. General McChrystal, who had once commanded the Ranger regiment, and earlier than that led its Second Battalion, felt left out. The airborne eventually got a piece of the action, but as security and support forces for logistics bases in Uzbekistan, and the first big US operating bases at Kandahar and Bagram. Each time Eighteenth Corps was asked to dispatch stripped-down combat teams tailored for the mission. It was only in May 2002 that McChrystal reached Afghanistan, when General McNeill and his headquarters deployed to lead all conventional US military operations in the country. By then it seemed the war was over. They were replacing Bert Calland's command, an act that represented the regular army taking the mantle back from SOF.

Paratroopers got their real chance when President George W. Bush launched his invasion of Iraq in March 2003. By then McChrystal, a major general, was a Pentagon planner. There he got a lesson of a different kind. One of the options prepared before the invasion involved neutralizing a Kurdish jihadist camp. The scheme was assigned to the US Special Operations Command, which selected one of its joint task forces to develop the option. The concept that came back called for a major incursion by SOF and supporting units. Pentagon skeptics groused that Special Forces weren't so "special" anymore. They couldn't do anything small. McChrystal recognized a variant of the classic antipathy between the conventional military and the shadow warriors. In Iraq he would get his chance to disprove the skeptics.

What Is a Joint Task Force?

The nomenclature for much special operations activity has become confusing. Back at the time of the Sontay raid and the Iranian hostage rescue the appellation "joint task force" was quite straightforward—an informal grouping of unconventional warfare assets from multiple armed services to accomplish a specified mission. Since then the usage has become more complex, particularly in the era following creation of the US Special Operations Command as one of the C-in-Cs. The continued existence of the Army Special Operations Command as a component of USSOCOM is confusing enough. The Joint Special Operations Command (JSOC) predated USSOCOM and continues today, as will be seen later, and it is a form of permanent joint task force. The JSOC carries out global missions the president gives to USSOCOM. Such an entity can be disguised by calling it a "task force." Through much of the last decade JSOC was known as Task Force 714. Then there are Special Operations Task Forces (SOTFs) that coordinate special operations for each of the regional C-in-Cs, utilizing forces provided them by USSOCOM. Any of these regional commands can create its own joint task force for a particular venture. The regional SOTFs would also provide local support and liaison for JSOC missions carried out in their areas. Meanwhile the SOTFs' own joint task forces, named or numbered, might be acting in the field alongside JSOC, under it or independently, and constitute virtual "units." The practice in the Iraq and Afghan wars of periodically switching the numbered joint task forces for security and operational reasons further complicates the situation. If this sounds confusing, it is. The best way to think of a "joint task force" today is as a field unit composed of shadow warriors drawn as required from all the different Special Operations Forces and even, where necessary, from other kinds of troops. In effect task forces are a new type of SOF unit that cuts across the traditional structure of USSOCOM formations.

What Happened after Tora Bora?

At a certain point the Afghan intervention morphed from a campaign into a war. Though Osama bin Laden and most of his al-Qaeda remnants had fled into Pakistan, followed by many of the Taliban jihadists, resistance did not disappear. More US conventional forces went to Afghanistan searching for the elusive enemy. Joint Task Force 180 replaced the earlier SOF-CIA command in charge of the action. Eventually there would be regional commands called task forces under the top leadership. The first big US battle of the war would be Operation Anaconda in the spring of 2002. SOF were active there, with a half dozen A-Teams, several SEAL elements, three air force special tactics teams, Nightstalker helicopters, a quick reaction force of Rangers, plus Australian Special Air Service troops. All formed parts of Joint Special Operations Task Force-South. All participated. The US commanders mounted an encirclement attempt against jihadi troops in a mountain valley, which led to a desperate fight between the enemy and the SEALs, who were attempting to establish observation posts on the peaks. One of the Nightstalkers was damaged and a SEAL fell out of the craft. This led to what is often called the battle of Roberts Ridge, for Petty Officer Neil Roberts, the sailor thrown from the chopper. There were strenuous efforts to find him. In addition to Roberts, never found, at least four SOF operators or Rangers died, and there were eleven wounded. Helicopters were lost or damaged. Worst, the jihadis escaped encirclement. Until 2006 Anaconda marked the most intense combat of the Afghan war. The routine became foot patrols or helicopter insertion for prescribed missions. Often as not SOF operators were assigned to call targets for air attack or observe the enemy around the fringes of a major NATO ground maneuver. This was long-range scouting in the classic style but in the rarified terrain of the Hindu Kush.

The Bush administration quickly shifted its gaze to Iraq and began to prepare an invasion of that country. Whether or not this was wise strategy, it had an immediate impact on Special Operations Forces worldwide. A variety of JSOC initiatives had to be curtailed to guarantee the adequacy of SOF resources for the invasion. In Afghanistan the ranks of the shadow warriors diminished by two-thirds or more. When the real history of the Afghan war is written one day, it will emerge that there was a moment, a tipping point, when the Western intervention had had the situation in hand, but through complacency proceeded to ignore the regeneration of the Taliban. That moment may well have been when SOF were drawn away for the Iraq invasion.

What Happened in Iraq?

Even as Operation Anaconda unfolded, in Washington President George W. Bush began planning to topple the dictator Saddam Hussein. The Iraq invasion began in March 2003. In the days after the attack the main SOF mission in Iraq was in the northern part of the country working with Kurdish tribal forces called the Peshmerga, a classic SOF mission. The Tenth Special Forces Group, a battalion from the Third, and an air contingent from the 352nd Special Operations Group, dubbed Task Force Viking, were the operating forces. More than fifty Operational Detachments Alpha (ODAs, the classic "A-Teams") were involved. In the 2003 invasion they were credited with tying down several Iraqi army divisions. When CENTCOM sent in the 173rd Airborne Brigade to furnish some hard muscle, it went under the task force's command. This marked the first time in American military history that SOF have controlled large conventional units. The northern campaign proved quite successful.

In the south A-Teams of the Fifth Group performed long-range scout missions and, as during the Gulf War, hunted for Scud missiles. At the outset of the invasion a strike force of SEALs, British Royal Marine commandos, and Polish SOF seized Iraqi offshore oil platforms in a direct attack. The Seventy-Fifth Rangers took objectives near Baghdad. Psychological warfare experts of the Ninth Psychological Warfare Battalion and 301st Company designed ploys to encourage Iraqi troops to surrender or defect, also quite successful. The invasion was quick. Images of Iraqi citizens pulling down statues of Saddam Hussein dominated the airwaves. Most SOF were redeployed very quickly, leaving only a skeleton force of fourteen ODAs in-country by July 2003. These withdrawn forces were not returned to Afghanistan but committed to fresh adventures in the global war on terror.

Special Forces provided some help in the search for Saddam's alleged weapons of mass destruction. That evolved into a pursuit-and-capture mission, plus civil affairs and psychological warfare. Many senior Iraqi generals, including Saddam himself, had escaped and gone to ground, and were hunted assiduously. The psy-war magicians came up with the fifty-five-card deck of playing cards, which became a curiosity for many Americans, and bore photos of the sought-after enemy who had been put on a "Black List." In guises such as Task Force 121, Task Force 16, Task Force 74, Task Force 714, and Task Force 6-26, Special Operations Forces were a mainstay in the hunt.

What Is Nodal Analysis?

Efforts to capture Saddam Hussein showcased new techniques for intelligence analysis. These methods melded the new eyes in the sky furnished by drones and the exotic capabilities of the electronic surveillance spectrum with the tradition of gumshoe eyeballing. Michael T. Flynn, at the time a staff officer, was a pioneer using these methods. Intelligence experts from SOF and the Fourth Infantry Division started with the known fact that Saddam came from a town called Tikrit. They began tracing family links to identify who might be helping the deposed Iraqi dictator, and posted patrols simply to watch the area. Flynn, then a colonel (today he is a general and heads the Defense Intelligence Agency), saw this as building a picture of the ebbs and flows of life in an area and coined the term "nodal analysis." Two months before Saddam's capture, SOF apprehended an individual who provided good leads, resulting in four more prisoners, one of whom revealed Saddam's actual hiding place. On December 13, 2003, regular troops surrounded the area, SOF reconnoitered the locations, and a combined unit found Saddam. Barely a day had passed since interrogators had obtained the key information. The operational style in Iraq—and Afghanistan too—featured unprecedented integration of SOF and conventional units, with the operators furnishing the intel and the regulars the troops to root out adversaries.

Why Didn't Saddam's Capture Stop the Insurgency?

Iraqi military forces faded after the US invasion. Many Iraqi troops, captured, were disbanded. Old army diehards provided the early resistance, but they were soon supplanted by Iraqis angry at the American occupation. The fight became one of tribal and religious rebels against the occupiers. Saddam Hussein had become a mere deposed leader, his capture a footnote to the evolving conflict. Al-Qaeda, the enemy of 9/11, began to pick up Iraqi jihadist allies, among whom a key leader was Abu Musab al-Zarqawi. The new figure was a great proponent of bombings. It is significant that the "improvised explosive device," the hallmark of this war, evolved on Zarqawi's watch and not that of Saddam. Senior

US officials, to include both President Bush and Secretary of Defense Donald Rumsfeld, eager to claim victory, ignored the early signs of rebellion. They proceeded to limit the number of US forces committed to Iraq in such a way that troops were thin on the ground. That opened the door for "private military contractors," who began to appear in combat zones in unprecedented numbers. It also made Special Operations Forces, however much reduced, the strong arm of the occupying army. With its intelligence techniques and ear to the ground, SOF was more aware of the rise of the insurgency, but its main operational tactic of night raids actually exacerbated the situation.

What about SOF and Torture?

This is a hard one. The need for intelligence involved SOF, and their interrogation methods became controversial as the result of charges of torture. The operational environment in Iraq (and Afghanistan) typically created situations where soldiers frustrated by improvised explosive devices (IEDs) and exhausted from the tensions of long approaches were taking prisoner men whose allegiances were not known. The soldiers had a deadline too—they had to put captives into the general prisoner population after a certain time if the Iraqis were not selected for special interrogation. And those who *were* specially interrogated were the objects of soldiers whose intel work had become closely integrated with SOF operations. That not only gave the interrogators a stake in "proving" their preliminary suspicions, it left prisoners at the mercy of men whose buddies were facing the IEDs every day. Plus the SOF interrogators had *continuing* access to the prisoners even after they were sent to other facilities.

General McChrystal swears that no prisoner was tortured, or at least that every overweening interrogator was promptly punished under his command. But Camp Nama, the Iraqi facility SOF used for interrogations, acquired a reputation as sinister as Bagram Prison in Afghanistan. Officers from other commands as well as monitors from the Judge Advocate General were blocked from entering Nama. Agents of the army's Criminal Investigations Division were denied jurisdiction. SOF basically stonewalled. Though US investigation claimed that Iraqi prisoners had fabricated accounts they gave the International Committee of the Red Cross and other investigators, thirty-four shadow warriors were nevertheless disciplined in some measure. At least a third of them were reassigned. Army Rangers were court-martialed (but received very light sentences). Members of a SEAL team were prosecuted when an Iraqi air force general they were interrogating died in their custody. More men were disciplined after revelation of the excesses at Abu Ghraib prison, which was not controlled by SOF but where operators had gone to question terrorist suspects. An army review, the Formica Report in 2005, concluded that while US techniques had been given proper review, the Joint Special Operations Task Force–Arabian Peninsula, and especially ODAs 554 and 065, should be given refresher training on human rights norms.

Who Killed al-Zarqawi?

On June 7, 2006, air force F-16 fighter-bombers dropped two smart bombs on a house near Baqubah. Al-Zarqawi was inside. It was a meeting place for the jihadists. Troops followed up on the ground and discovered the al-Qaeda commander. It is disputed whether Zarqawi was already dead, died from his wounds, or succumbed from a beating. But the backstory is like the saga of Saddam Hussein: a long hunt by SOF and other troops, a gradual closing in, careful observation of the target location, and a final strike.

The story begins in Fallujah, the city in the western Iraqi province of Anbar that would become the focus of major battles, ambitions, and frustrations in the Iraq war. In February 2004, a few months after assuming command of the global spec ops counterterror group called Task Force 714, Major General Stanley McChrystal went on a night raid with men of his task force who fought in Iraq. Unbeknownst to McChrystal, Abu Musab al-Zarqawi was less than a block away. McChrystal's operators were intent on taking down a house they thought was an enemy base. Nothing. If Zarqawi had been there, he escaped. SOF searched other houses. Nothing there either. McChrystal could see the fear and hate on the faces of the Iraqi civilians whose homes were being invaded. He realized that SOF needed better intelligence. The night raids were a staple of SOF tactics in this war, but they were also a major negative in peoples' attitudes toward the Americans. Targeting raids more precisely could reduce their adverse effect.

General McChrystal created a new operations center for his overall command that he called the "situational awareness center," as well as the Iraq-focused Task Force 16. This was the center for Mike Flynn's nodal analysis. Physically it resembled a traditional newspaper newsroom (an open-plan office space), or, perhaps taking into account the wall of screens displaying developing operations and intelligence information, a NASA launch or operations facility. Staff experts put a grid over a map of Iraq and divided it into areas of interest, then began systematically collecting information about each one. McChrystal applied similar methods at a global level for his larger arena of activity. The idea was to tear down compartmentalization and facilitate the exchange of information, rather the opposite of standard SOF practice, which the general believed had slowed and hampered effective action.

This painstaking assemblage of information progressively built a more detailed picture of jihadist efforts. SOF intelligence experts identified "ratlines" the militants were using to move foreign fighters into Iraq, and they discovered when Zarqawi shifted his pattern of operations. Early in 2006 SOF captured a jihadist bomb expert they knew as one of Zarqawi's lieutenants, and he identified a safe house in one of Task Force 16's areas of interest. The operators began to watch it with aerial assets, and strike teams went after the safe house when the enemy were seen meeting there, then after another house where some jihadists had fled as the first place came under attack. A dozen men captured at the second house turned out to be al-Qaeda leaders, including some senior commanders and couriers. One of them identified Zarqawi's spiritual adviser, whom the operators followed, from the air and on the ground, for more than two weeks. This man finally led them to the place where Zarqawi lay hidden, and the air strikes were called when SOF decided the jihadist might escape a raiding mission.

Information from detainees also led Task Force 16 to Zarqawi's replacement, killed in a joint raid with Iraqi troops in the spring of 2010. General McChrystal insists that none of his SOF operators ever used so-called enhanced interrogation techniques, and that all questioning followed only the official field manual. In any case, while the air force may lay claim to the neutralization of Abu Musab al Zarqawi, Special Operations Forces deserve a large share of the credit.

How Effective Were the Night Raids?

General Stanley McChrystal thought of night raids as devices to gather intel on the enemy, bringing back captives who would divulge information. Enough of that and SOF could target the networks, hopefully effectively enough to dismantle them. In Iraq in 2004 SOF were mounting eighteen raids a month. A couple of years later they were doing that many in two days. The use of the tactic increased in Afghanistan as well, especially once Stanley McChrystal arrived there as commander of the multinational forces in the summer of 2009. For the first time in the Afghan war the general also brought the SOF in-country task forces under his direct command. By his account McChrystal worked to change the strategic thrust from fighting the Taliban to protecting the population. It was an approach that complemented CENTCOM's counterinsurgency emphasis.

Much like the SOF shift from combat missions to peace operations in the 1990s, tactics remained pretty much the same. As he had done in Iraq, McChrystal sought to increase the use of intelligence-directed raids. But in accentuating the night raids, he injected a contradictory element into the technique. As McChrystal had himself seen in Iraq, the people hated these raids, so any security gains from eliminating bad guys were in danger of being canceled by an increasingly sullen and resentful population aiding the enemy. The Iraq war ended, and the major portion of the NATO and US withdrawal from Afghanistan is underway, but fighting in both places continues and is intensifying. Neither conflict outcome appears to have been determined by the raids.

A command shuffle General McChrystal triggered by blundering dealings with journalists brought his replacement in the summer of 2010. But the emphasis on night raids remained—and the Afghans became more and more restive. Afghan president Hamid Karzai began to denounce quite regularly both allied air strikes, which led to civilian deaths, and the night raids, which regularly swept up innocents along with any Taliban they captured. As Afghan military forces increased and became more proficient, allied commanders tried to smooth the sharp edges of this issue by including Afghan troops in the night missions. But SOF took the lead even when the raids were joint ones.

Karzai's complaints continued. In 2013 the international security force reversed the tactical method. Now the NATO Special Forces hung back while Afghan troops led. That resulted in less effective raids, however. For the most important missions American or allied SOF were still in front, but for the vast majority of operations the Afghans had the command. Shadow warriors held primary responsibility for what were called "village stability operations" in fifty-seven districts of the country. The SOF also pitched in to help CIA train and lead a new-style paramilitary force, the "Afghan Local Police," in part to create an action mechanism outside the Afghan government–International Security Assistance Force framework. By 2012 there were 11,000 of these paramilitary troops.

By then the Obama administration and NATO had declared their intention to withdraw most allied forces from Afghanistan, leaving behind a residual force to help train the Afghan military and—equally important—continue SOF direct action strikes. At this point night raids actually became a sticking point in the negotiations for an international agreement to cover the missions of the foreign troops and their status under Afghan law. As the talks became more contentious the American and allied plans for a residual force were pared back. At this writing it appears that night raids will not long survive the departure of the major American force in the country.

On balance it seems night raiding tactics have been a double-edged sword. They have been effective when supporting a robust conventional force in a relatively stable pacification environment as in Iraq. In Afghanistan, in the context of a deteriorating situation, the night raids, whatever their military impact, have challenged the relationship with the host country. The result may well be a net negative but since the NATO withdrawal is not yet complete and the war is ongoing at this writing, the jury is still out.

Did the Iraq and Afghan Wars Oblige SOF to Change or Refine Their Practices and Doctrines?

Yes. The old standard of the direct action mission—a commando raid, say, to take over an Iranian oil platform or to simulate an invasion of the Iraqi coast—amounted to a carefully planned sally by SOF to seize and control, or to destroy, an objective. These missions were finite. While there might be a series of sallies like that, they did not amount to constant patrols by small groups of troopers. Now the patrols and the night raids became standard tactical activity. In addition there have been changes in the SOF intelligence approach exemplified by General McChrystal's situational awareness center. Though Special Operations Forces activities have always had a strong intelligence component, the texture of that has changed. Standard practices used to be aimed at shielding needed information within a very small contingent, "need to know." The more recent approach, fueled by the necessity of informing massive numbers of small-scale operations, is to share intelligence more widely.

Special Forces operations historically have had a tendency to become famous or notorious individually—and at times long afterward. Thus the discussions that have raged over certain Vietnam missions, the Iran hostage rescue, the Pablo Escobar killing, or the battle of Mogadishu. The old exception was the "Phoenix" program. Now it appears that SOF activities have become controversial across the board and almost immediately. Torture charges, the night raids, and the drone war are all in this group. How SOF deals with the controversies may have much to do with its future status in the US military.

The nature of warfare has also imposed changes. The IED, in a thousand forms and every imaginable disguise, affected Special Operations Forces as it did all others. A stealthy insertion of strike teams became nearly impossible when the operators were forced to hunker down in widely separated (but protected) bases, and deploy over long distances by means of high-speed motor convoys, slow but heavily armored transport vehicles, or by noisy helicopter flights. One study shows that from 2001 to 2004, eighty-two SOF operators died in the war on terror, nearly 80 percent of them in combat. Of those, nearly half were due to explosions. Another medical study identified 225 Special Forces wounded in Iraq between the invasion and October 2007 and shows a consistent pattern. Head wounds and those to the lower extremities—common in IED incidents, accounted for 72 percent of the casualties all by themselves. The studies are not exactly comparable since the second does not identify causes of wounds, but the data are suggestive. The US military procured new carrier vehicles that are hardened against IEDs but heavier and slower. USSOCOM ordered several hundred of these vehicles in 2007.

Traditional methods are still employed. The bin Laden raid was a direct action in the classic style. But the majority of SOF activity has been dedicated to security operations, like the night raids, not (as in Vietnam) to territorial security or lurp operations. There have also been very few prisoners taken in the wars, so POW rescue has ceased to be a focus. And Special Forces A-Teams have been primarily engaged in training and advising the Afghan army and police, not pacification duty or mobilizing local militias. The rescue function of SOF is also fully active: in the spring of 2014, when the Taliban released their single American prisoner from the Afghan war, Sergeant Bowe Bergdahl, it was a team of SOF who met the jihadis near the Pakistani border to retrieve the POW and spirit him away on a helicopter.

What Is the Marine Special Operations Command?

For a long time the Marine Corps resisted jumping on the unconventional warfare bandwagon. The Corps preferred to think that *all* its forces are "special operations" forces, and that it has an inherent capability for this type of effort. But its standing formations had been allowed to atrophy. By the 1990s there was a Force Reconnaissance Company in place of two battalions, and recon platoons rather than companies within marine divisions. Given the numerous humanitarian and peacemaking operations of that decade, the Corps felt a need to do more, and made a start by trying to maintain a higher readiness for immediate operations within some of its deployed Marine Expeditionary Units. A joint study group of marine and SOCOM officers formed to consider more far-reaching changes, but nothing was done. In the mid-1990s interest petered out.

The September 11 attacks revived the study group, and several new entities followed. A "Marine SOCOM Detachment" cooperated with SEALs in the Iraq invasion, carrying out two dozen direct action missions as well as strategic recons. The Corps created a Fourth Marine Expeditionary Brigade (MEB) and gave it a counterterrorism specialization. Its Foreign Military Training Unit, which did work similar to Green Beret mobile training units, would be regrouped under the Fourth MEB. In February 2006 the Corps created the Marine Special Operations Command (MARSOC) and joined SOCOM.

Seeking a more coherent force structure the Corps next created the Marine Special Operations Regiment with three battalions. Marines of the Fourth MEB, several Force Reconnaissance platoons, and the Foreign Military Training Unit were incorporated into the new regiment. The first operational deployment was to Afghanistan's Farwah province in the summer of 2009 for Operation Red Thunder, an effort to restore security around Shewan village. General McChrystal would acclaim this as amazing work. As of March 2010 there were nearly 2,300 assigned to the Marine Special Operations Command, including 124 civilians and 180 sailors. Two-thirds of the regiment remains focused on the Afghan war. The marines are experimenting with a mixed task force structure in which a Marine SOF company controls a SEAL platoon, a few Green Beret A-Teams, and a regular troop battalion, very much along the lines of the force used in Red Thunder. Training Afghan local forces and supervising the transition to Afghan-led operations, marines are beginning to talk about "combat diplomacy."

Did the Wars Change Special Forces' Relationship with the CIA?

Yes, for reasons of interservice competition as well as the jealousies of senior officials, the post-9/11 wars have widened the cleavages that separate SOF from the intelligence services. In the initial response after the 9/11 attacks, only the CIA had preexisting links to Afghan opposition groups with whom the

United States wanted to ally. The CIA was also prepared to move instantly, whereas the military took a little bit longer.

Defense secretary Donald Rumsfeld did not like ceding primacy to the civilian intelligence agency. Rumsfeld wanted military spies, provocateurs, and operators who had no CIA agenda. To get them he seemed willing to cut back on traditional SOF roles. For example, conventional troops began to participate in training foreign militaries, a role that had been the preserve of the SOF mobile training team. Rumsfeld took steps to employ increasing numbers of SOF in clandestine espionage and operational roles, including undercover in countries where the State Department and CIA were left in ignorance of the military activity. Secretary Rumsfeld viewed such activities as preparing the battlefield. Since after 9/11 the "battlefield" was defined as the entire world, the defense secretary was effectively setting up his unconventional warriors as another kind of CIA.

Vice President Richard Cheney was supportive of this course. The vice president favored developments that increased the capacity of the United States to act on the global stage. Cheney also chaffed at restrictions that limited executive action. The military and the CIA each operated under different sets of laws. Title 10 of the US code controlled military actions, premised on large-scale activities subject to numerous strictures; Title 50, governing the CIA, presupposes limited activities subject to very modest oversight. Having entities with operational capabilities on both sides of the legal code afforded the administration unprecedented flexibility. The Bush White House could, in effect, select which set of laws it wanted to have applied to a certain activity and then order the CIA or JSOC to take the desired actions. White House decisions to forge ahead under one set of laws or the other affected the SOF-CIA relationship when either the spooks or the operators thought the activities were exclusively in their portfolios.

One example that will be examined in greater detail shortly is the case of the drone war. The unmanned aircraft, originally developed by the air force for reconnaissance, were first used in an attack mode by the CIA. For several years the agency owned the drone war. Then JSOC arrived to take up the cudgel and the shoe was on the other foot.

Thus, as with SOF and the regular military, the SOF-CIA relationship since 9/11 has been very close at times but marked with discomfort in other situations. Some unconventional warfare operators view CIA's quasi-military involvements across the globe as competition with their own mission. The agency's monopoly on action in Pakistan can be framed as not fully supporting US military efforts in Afghanistan. Conversely, some at CIA deplore the extent to which their agency has become militarized since the "SMO" days of the 1990s, and would prefer to cede the role to the Special Operations Forces, returning to their classic focus of spying. The SOF-CIA relationship should be viewed as cyclical. At this writing it appears the trend is toward increased distance, with the emphasis on CIA intelligence support and less agency operational involvement. But the cycle can reverse itself readily.

How about SOF and the Private Military Contractors?

Another dilemma exists in the relationship between Special Operations Forces and "private military contractors," or "private security companies," terms currently favored for fighters known in other eras as *condottieri*, mercenaries or soldiers of fortune. There have always been soldiers of fortune, and there have always been veterans ready to enlist in the private ventures. Since the creation of Special Forces there has been a steady percolation of former operators into the private contractor ranks. But this phenomenon seems to have become especially thorny in the war on terror, not so much because of SOF but because the services of the private contractors have been very much in demand, and their recruiters offer very attractive terms to shadow warriors who, of course, are among the most highly skilled military men.

Probably not since the wars of the Renaissance have soldiers of fortune had such a large role in conflicts. Sheer numbers tell the story: in Iraq American fighting strength peaked at 140,000, British at 9,000, and a kaleidoscope of minor allies added perhaps another 30,000. The private companies moved in early and mushroomed. Dozens of companies were involved, the number of hired guns going to 12,000, then 20,000, then estimates of 48,000, 100,000, even one of more than the number of regular troops. Precise numbers are impossible to pin down, but were certainly the equivalent of a small army. In Afghanistan in 2010 there were more than fifty firms with some 25,000 troops. At that time, just at the outset of the Obama "surge," there were 68,000 US regulars. If not US forces as a whole, the private contractors certainly outnumbered SOF.

Extra guns might have been merely a good thing, except for other factors. The hired guns were not in the US—nor NATO, nor allied—chain of command. They had their own rules and their distinct brand of discipline and behavior. The company called Blackwater (then Xe, now Academi) got the contract to protect US commissioner Paul Bremer, its launching platform in Iraq. Blackwater put seventy-eight people in place just for that and soon had many more. It was the March 2004 deaths of four Blackwater operators that ignited the first battle of Fallujah, the fiercest of the Iraq war. In September 2007 a Blackwater security detail transiting Nissour Square in Baghdad opened fire at civilians, killing seventeen and wounding twenty more people. The company insisted its operators were not subject to Iraqi laws and got them out of the country. Actions by contractors had concrete effects on populations—motivating civilians to take sides and to join an enemy that SOF and regular troops then had to fight.

In Afghanistan in December 2009 several of the Americans killed in the suicide bomb attack on the CIA's Forward Operating Base Chapman were contractor employees, including two with Blackwater, among them Jeremy Wise, the thirty-seventh Blackwater battle death of the wars. Thus the private security companies were accumulating extensive casualty lists of their own. Jeremy Wise had previously been a SEAL with Naval Special Warfare Group 2. President Hamid Karzai had complained for a while about the mercenaries, but he eventually went further—in October 2010 Karzai banned the activities of all contractors not licensed by the Afghan government.

American regulars were spread thinly on the ground in both Iraq and Afghanistan. In other places across the globe there was even less of a US presence. But there were still jobs to be done ranging from protecting VIPs and key physical plants, to general security, to specialized functions like protecting merchant ships from pirates, which gained importance with the persistence of pirate nests in Somalia and Southeast Asia over the past decade. Jobs in private security were readily available to former SOF operators, and they paid handsomely. Special Forces operators had friends sprinkled through the private contractor community, thus reasons for a favorable attitude toward it.

A tragic, if poignant example is the merchant vessel *Maersk Alabama*. In April 2009, en route down the Red Sea from Djibouti to Mombasa on the east coast of Africa, the ship was accosted by Somali pirates. Confronted by US warships, the pirates fled in a lifeboat, taking the ship's captain, Richard Phillips, with them. Sharpshooters of SEAL Team Six, firing from the fantail of the destroyer *Bainbridge*, ended the incident, killing all three pirates then holding Captain Phillips, whom they rescued. For shipping companies, the lesson was "get protection." They hired private contractors. Two former operators, Jeffrey Reynolds (SEAL Team Five) and Mark D. Kennedy (Teams Two and Eight), were in the Indian Ocean aboard the very same ship, *Maersk Alabama*, when she docked at Port Victoria in the Seychelles Islands in February 2014. They had mustered out of the navy and worked for the Trident Group, a Virginia contractor. Both ex-SEALs were found dead aboard the ship. Family and comrades reject the version that attributes their deaths to drugs and alcohol. In any case, Reynolds and Kennedy serve to illustrate the ability of SOF fighters to move readily into the security business.

What Is the Role of Special Forces in Drone Warfare?

The US Special Operations Command has acquired a big piece of the drone attack mission by somewhat circuitous means. The idea of SOF operators working the controls of remotely piloted unmanned aerial vehicles is quite novel. A different way to put this question might be, "How the hell did Joint Special Operations Command wind up flying drones, anyway?" Unlike commando attacks, night raids, long-range scout missions, or even gunship sorties, the drone flights involve *only* distant actions and seem the very antithesis of "special operations." The mission evolved in the following way.

The air force developed long-endurance unmanned aerial vehicles (UAV) in competition with the CIA starting from the 1980s. The agency preferred a small-airframe UAV and was first off the mark. The air force's larger and stealthy vehicles were longer in development. The CIA's craft became the "Predator" that is so well known today. The United States first deployed Predators in 1995 to the Balkans, where they served strictly as surveillance vehicles and were piloted by army/ navy crews using equipment vans located at the airfields where drones were launched. Meanwhile the air force worked on mating the Predator UAV with the "Hellfire" missile, a combination perfected in the summer of 2001. Originally designed to destroy Russian heavy tanks, Hellfires gave the Predator a significant punch. When the 9/11 attacks brought US action in Afghanistan, Washington made a deal with Pakistan to permit Predator flights into Afghanistan from a Pakistani base. The CIA flew the first armed Predator mission into Afghan country on October 7, 2001.

So far, no Special Forces. They came in as the use of the drones expanded. About six months into the program, flight missions began in Yemen, and the CIA eliminated an al-Qaeda leader there. At the Pentagon Donald Rumsfeld issued orders that made the US Special Operations Command an actual field command, acting through its Joint Special Operations Command (JSOC) for global counterterrorism operations. That—plus the Pentagon's insistence that it could better act in theaters like the Yemen or the Horn of Africa—won JSOC its Predator spurs. The mission grew slowly at first because the United States soon invaded Iraq and for many months afterward demands for drones to support the Iraq occupation forces absorbed most of the military capacity. But from the middle of the decade onward, when the larger "Reaper" drones also began to enter the force, capacity broadened and more of the mission went to JSOC.

When Barack Obama became president in 2009 he was enamored of the drones, seeing them as ideal instruments for the United States to act without overtly violating diplomatic customs. At that point the Joint Special Operations Command's role in the drone war became major, with actual bases constructed in Djibouti, leased in the Seychelles, and created in conjunction with the CIA in Saudi Arabia.

Of course, simply to say that "JSOC flies drones" is an oversimplification. Operations can involve both air strikes and troops, as was the case with "Celestial Balance" in Somalia in September 2009. In this case, instead of a drone, an air-launched missile was supposed to take out a Kenyan jihadi who had been involved in the bombing of US embassies in Africa back in the Clinton administration. He was thought to be the link between al-Qaeda and the Somali Islamist groups. But the missile launcher malfunctioned. The fallback plan had been to have SEALs standing by, and that was the final solution. Helicopters strafed the bad guy's road convoy and killed him.

By 2011 the intelligence agency and JSOC were together on some missions and in other cases arranging which ops should be "Title 10" versus "Title 50" forays. In 2013, when John O. Brennan became CIA director, the talk was about rededicating the agency to its classic tradecraft and spy mission, getting it out of the drone business altogether. Agency officers are concerned about the degree to which the CIA has become militarized. But JSOC is unable to take up the CIA's reins in Pakistan, where the US military is prohibited from operating. And within the agency the apparatus for special operations is well funded and highly developed after a decade of investment. Brennan's talk has not led to CIA action. The probability is the agency and the JSOC will both continue in the drone campaign.

Are There "Special Targets"?

Yes. This war began with the leaders of the al-Qaeda terrorists, and a list of key enemies soon appeared in a sort of "FBI Most Wanted List" format. George W. Bush wanted them dead or alive. Then there were the playing cards after the Iraq invasion. The CIA is known to approve target folders, which identify individuals, make a case for why they should be neutralized, and collect the information required to target them. Osama bin Laden was the most important, and they got him in 2011, but Zarqawi was once on that list, as was the American citizen Anwar al-Alaki. It was a matter of a policy decision for President Obama whether to restrict the Predators to the stipulated targets or permit attack on classes of objects—"signature strikes"—aimed, for example, at groups of young men seen carrying guns (not uncommon in that part of the world). The Pentagon has an actual list it updates at weekly conferences. Special targets have been the subject of White House meetings. As we saw earlier, the bin Laden raid occasioned precisely that kind of presidential attention.

Early in 2004 Secretary Rumsfeld approved a Pentagon order with respect to its target list. The Rumsfeld order made the Joint Special Operations Command the Pentagon's executive agent for global operations against the targets on that list. JSOC can use any weapon in the US arsenal to get at designated enemies anywhere in the world. The Rumsfeld order was what really got the Command into the drone business, and it has never let go. In Somalia JSOC has both used drones and carried out direct actions. It fueled an Ethiopian intervention into Somalia at one point, in hopes a friendlier faction might overcome the Islamists. In Uganda JSOC detachments have been aiding that nation's forces against the Lord's Resistance Army and its warlord Joseph Kony, another special target. Ground action was avoided in Yemen, where JSOC only used Predators. Special Forces have worked for JSOC in Indonesia, the Philippines, Niger, and Colombia, among other places, and in all of them drones or their equivalent have also been used for surveillance. The Joint Special Operations Command maneuvers to maximize the possibility of getting at special targets. Operations under General McChrystal and Admiral McRaven involved small detachments at the tip of the spear, but with full US support behind them. In aggregate the Command's missions field thousands of US soldiers, sailors, airmen, and marines.

What Are the Moral and Legal Implications of Identifying "Special Targets?"

An essential controversy has developed over the question of special targets. This comes into focus best when looked at in terms of Americans, but the moral and legal implications of attacking individuals, absent either a state of war or a judicial proceeding, permeates the issue of "special targeting." The idea of eliminating people on a "hit list" is distasteful. Is it criminal? Perhaps. The Geneva Conventions make murder in war a crime.

The same set of issues had touched the Special Operations Forces before, during the Vietnam War, with the notorious Phoenix program. Then the target had been the so-called "Viet Cong infrastructure." Any strategy that put emphasis on special targets placed a heavy burden on intelligence—you had to know the "bad guy" was for real, that his elimination would set back the enemy, and have high confidence on both counts. The United States had had trouble with that in Vietnam, but in the war on terror, where there is, if anything, even less direct contact with the adversary, authorities repeatedly claimed specific results—to have eliminated particular individuals among the terrorist hierarchy. Special Operations Forces had been burned in the fires of Vietnam controversies—not just Phoenix but the Green Beret Affair (when Special Forces troopers were court-martialed for the murder of an agent under their control)—and there were echoes again in Central America in the 1980s, where peasants in El Salvador and Honduras had been endangered by militaries that US Special Forces advised. Operators had no desire to fall into these kinds of controversies. One purpose of their extensive intelligence net is to make sure every special target amounts to a real enemy.

Unfortunately it's not possible to separate the neutralization action from its moral and legal aspects. Once the instrument for guidance becomes a target list, however compiled, the boundary line is already crossed. International law contains explicit definitions for who is a "combatant"—and therefore an object for lethal action. But SOF are not facing uniformed and organized enemy troops in the field. Their special targets are rarely uniformed and are most often encountered at home—as bin Laden was taken—in camp, in a vehicle, or in some other nonthreatening circumstance.

Government authorities argue the nature of the war as the basis for the legality of their actions. That the conflict is against so-called nonstate actors that (mostly) lack constituted armies (beyond informal bands of fighters) is true. It is also accurate that the terrorist enemy is capable of violence. But it is less clear that the adversary poses a direct and imminent threat to the United States, which is what the authorities rely upon. In addition the employment of indirect means of action, such as the JSOC Predator, adds an extra layer of uncertainty to any action. The Zarqawi-type "hit," where SOF had eyes on the target for a considerable time prior to swinging into action, is more the exception than the rule. This is particularly true now, when both military and CIA are permitted to attack signature targets—no longer even names on a list.

The conundrums of legality emerge most clearly when the subject is Americans made into special targets. Starting with Anwar al-Awlaki, killed in September 2011, Americans have been special targets. Since the start of the war on terror half a dozen Americans—innocents or special targets (or people siding with the enemy but yet to be declared special targets)— have perished at the tip of JSOC or CIA Predators. The problem is that American nationals automatically enjoy constitutional protections. The Fourth and Fifth Amendments are supposed to shield Americans from loss of life, unreasonable search and seizure, and more, except on the basis of a trial where they may confront their accusers before a jury of citizens with a judge and evidentiary rules. Of course no such legal niceties exist with Predator strikes, where the hit list functions as a death warrant and there has been no court proceeding whatever. At this moment news reports indicate the Obama administration is considering adding another American to the hit list, a bomb maker known as Abdullah al Shami, believed to be hiding in Pakistan.

Authorities have cobbled together some pretty arcane arguments in their effort to preserve some impression of legality here. The constitutional breach is self-evident. Operators or CIA agents are substituting for judge, jury, and executioner—*and*, it should be added, substituting intelligence data for court-accepted evidence. The legal arguments now hinge even more strongly on assertions that American special targets are "imminent" and "significant" threats, and also on the contention that capturing these Americans and sending them to trial is not possible. The latter claim is based on the alleged difficulty of mounting capture missions and seems contrived. After all, McRaven's operators could pursue Osama bin Laden himself into the heart of Pakistan. Equally to the point, SEALs openly raided Tripoli, Libya, in October 2013 to snatch a man suspected as a plotter of the bombings of US embassies in Kenya and Tanzania that took place in 1998.

The legal controversies that surround SOF action against special targets will continue. At this writing the United Nations and the European Union have both expressed dismay over these tactics, and the UN has begun an investigation that may end with criminal charges against American JSOC warriors or CIA officers. Foreign public groups have filed an actual complaint with the International Criminal Court. Criminal charges may or may not result, but it is safe to predict that we are witnessing the beginning of a drive to create new international law of war to govern either the utilization of target lists of individuals or the employment of remote-controlled direct strike weapons such as the Predator—or both.

6

WHAT FUTURE FOR THE "ARMY OF ONE"?

ABSTRACT

As Special Operations Forces face the future, there are tensions that start with the United States leaving the Afghan war, and with the continuing dilemmas of US economic problems. The Pentagon budget is already in decline, and a key issue is where the point comes that SOF must share in the cuts. In that environment Special Forces may desire to expand *their roles as a mechanism for preserving their slice of the budget. A larger SOF role depends both on the shape of future conflicts—unpredictable—and the balance of political power between the SOF and other armed services branches. There may also be roles, such as the drone war, that SOF might prefer to discard. For the moment SOF continue to expand and continue to perform their classic missions, although there are hints in SOCOM future planning that it expects a reduction in force. If you want to be a Special Forces operator, you should expect to confront big challenges along the way. Here the text outlines some of the SOF training programs.*

What Tensions Exist within the Special Operations Community Today?

Tensions exist, and some of them are over SOF roles. The shape of the next great conflict matters. If it is a war with, say China, over Chinese adventures across the Pacific Rim, American leaders are going to require major conventional forces to confront the People's Republic. Aircraft carriers and bombers and divisions of troops will be at the center. The SOF will have a role to play on the margins, with direct action missions, but SOCOM's importance will be very different from what it has been in the war on terror. If the next conflict is like Afghanistan, the individual expert operator, the "Army of One," will continue to be preeminent. If we look at the international sore points of the moment, it is difficult to hazard a guess. For every China or Russia, there is a Syria or Somalia.

Counterterror operations will continue even as the Afghan war ends. Some officers think the Joint Special Operations Command is overcommitted or else engaged in ways that may rebound against the shadow warriors. Drone warfare is a novelty in terms of SOF missions, and has more to do with desired secrecy and legal authorities than with Special Forces per se. The Joint Special Operations Command had the counterterror assignment and the drone was considered an appropriate weapon. But as the number of, utility of, and demands for the drones increase, it is likely that other branches of the armed services will want more slices of the task, and may well take it away. Meanwhile the controversies over target lists and signature strikes must discomfit JSOC as well. Legality of the drone attacks is a continuing issue at both the domestic and international levels, and there is a potential for war crimes charges to flow from this program. The shadow warriors may prefer to unload this mission, so very remote from their self-image of ultimate hands-on operators.

At the time of this writing, May 2014, President Obama has declared the end of 2016 as the date when the last US troops will exit the Afghan war, whether or not it is over. Delivering the commencement address for young officers graduating from West Point, the president articulated his vision for the next phase: Obama stresses that terrorism remains the main threat to America abroad and at home, "But a strategy that involves invading every country that harbors terrorist networks is naïve and unsustainable."[1] The president wants to rely upon cooperation with local allies, where US forces will take "direct action"—Mr. Obama used the precise SOF term of art—when there is good intelligence. This is clearly a strategy that affords broad scope for the Army of One.

Meanwhile there are tensions that arise from social developments. Repeated and dangerous deployments put strains on SOF families. When promulgating a new long-range vision for his command, called "SOCOM 2020," Admiral McRaven specifically noted that "USSOCOM must ensure our SOF warriors and their families are properly cared for by reducing the stress they face from the lack of predictability and demanding operational tempos exacerbated by significant time spent away from home."[2] Initiatives to increase time at home between deployments are in the works. The easiest solution depends on having a larger force. That has its own difficulties too.

Tensions revolve around the Special Operations Forces' lengthy rise. Since the 1980s the Special Forces have more or less constantly been building up. The traditional disparities between conventional and unconventional forces remain in play. In fiscal year 2012 USSOCOM reported an aggregate strength of 66,100 soldiers. The army has been adding a battalion of Green Berets to each of its five active Special Forces groups and expected to complete the force increase in 2012. SOCOM also added an SOF-specialized logistics unit called a "sustainment brigade." Admiral McRaven, in congressional testimony at that time, anticipated achieving a force goal of 71,100 troopers by 2015. Currently, on any given day some 12,000 SOF troops are forward deployed in an average of seventy countries.

Meanwhile overall US military strength is slated to decline in the wake of Iraq and Afghanistan, with planned army reductions of about 27,000 soldiers, and marine strength cuts of between 15,000 and 20,000. Since SOF draws upon the armed services for its operators, there is a question whether its growth goals can be achieved or the force sustained. Pentagon budgets have begun to decline. The US military anticipates some troop reductions in the wake of ending wars in Iraq and Afghanistan. So far the USSOCOM budget has continued to increase, but at some point cuts must affect SOF. In his SOCOM 2020 vision statement McRaven acknowledged as much—reporting that the chairman of the Joint Chiefs of Staff has issued strategic guidance instructing commands to maintain troop readiness and capability in preference to attempting to preserve an existing force structure. Conventionally minded officers may be expected to protest if SOF gets a pass while the regular forces absorb the burden of reductions.

The Special Forces' preference will be to absorb *more* roles and missions as a device to preserve SOCOM strength at existing levels within a smaller American military. It's far from clear if this ploy can work, and it diverges from the idea of getting JSOC out of the drone business. But new roles could preserve SOF force structure. The marines' study of their postwar force, for example, envisions increasing the Marine Special Operations Command by a thousand troops, a one-third increase. In his 2012 testimony Admiral McRaven referred to an exponential rise in the number and scope of threats.[3] Viewed from today's perspective, with wars ending and the United States reluctant to commit to new conflicts, but a fresh enemy manifesting itself in Syria and Iraq, McRaven might be right. On the other hand the "long war" on terror has lost some of its intensity, and with the Islamist caliphate in Syria so far focused internally, the threat may not be increasing at all.

Meanwhile Special Forces continue to operate in their classic roles. In the summer and fall of 2013, when violence engulfed the Central African Republic and French troops plus African Union forces were sent in to restore order, SOCOM helped with the airlift. In places as diverse as Kenya and Mali, SOF lead the way by providing intelligence support plus military training for national armies. But there is new competition. The Africa Command, latest of the US military's regional C-in-Cs, has struggled with the limitation that practically all its resources *were* SOF. Aside from warships patrolling against

Somali pirates, reconnaissance drone operators at a base in Niger, and marines on temporary deployment in Djibouti, all the Command's operating elements have been SOF. When jihadis attacked the American consulate in Benghazi, Libya, back in the fall of 2012, there were no regular US troops to respond to the emergency, and aircraft, drones, and SOF were in no position to react. It is not coincidental that since then, for the first time, a brigade of the First Infantry Division has been designated for Africa missions, including many of the same kinds of training activities that were long the province of SOF. Its current ventures range the gamut from humanitarian initiatives in South Africa to a two-man sniper team on service in Burundi. This may represent the opening wedge of a bid from the conventional forces to get a share of Special Forces' roles.

Another good example of SOF in their classic role is the double-pronged raid that took place in Africa on October 5, 2013. In that action, Delta Force operators infiltrated Tripoli, in Libya, to apprehend a suspect wanted since the 1998 terrorist bombings of two US embassies. The snatch-and-grab mission was a success. At the same time SEALs came from the sea off the Somali coastal town of Baraawe in a nighttime raid intended to capture a senior member of the Shahab Islamist movement, which has been on JSOC's target list in Somalia. The raid spun out of control when Somali guards saw the SEALs and opened fire. The raiders returned fire and, having lost the element of surprise, withdrew to their boats.

Force protection is a key interest. Spotlighting this aspect is an April 24, 2014, incident in a barbershop in Sanaa, the capital of Yemen, where an SOF operator and a CIA officer confronted two armed men believed to be part of an al-Qaeda kidnapping ring. The Americans shot both Yemenis to death. As with Kenya, Yemen is one of those countries where mobile training teams are being sent to prepare local forces to cope with threats in their countries. The April incident reminds us that about fifty Special Forces troopers have gone to Yemen in recent years.

In recent conflict situations—Syria and the Ukraine—SOF would have been suitable for preparing local forces the United States decided to support. The mobile training teams could accomplish much. However, against either the Syrian army or the Russian army in a Ukraine contingency, Special Operations Forces lack the weight and firepower to contest the battlefield by themselves. The key in many situations, as it has been in Afghanistan, is the relationship with allies. Brigadier General Edward M. Reeder Jr., the current commander of US Army Special Forces, says he has done five Afghan tours leading SOF and *never* executed a US unilateral operation. That sounds very much like an exaggeration—it might be believable if the presence of an interpreter changed the nature of the mission to "multilateral," but the point stands that cooperation with allies is vital.

Do Special Forces Return to Places They Have Left?

Most certainly. Some of the discomfort surrounding plans for the US withdrawal from Afghanistan, and the diplomatic dance with the Afghan government over a status-of-forces agreement that would govern the activities of an American residual force flow precisely from this kind of concern. Some generals and politicians prefer a residual force—especially one endowed with SOF strike capabilities—to leaving the country but facing a potential need for renewed commitment later.

This sort of phenomenon is evident in the case of Somalia. Following the intervention of 1992 there have been several subsequent occasions where SOF have been sent back into the country. Early in this century there were support missions for an Ethiopian army intervening against Somali jihadists, then direct strike missions by Americans against extremist groups. In the period since 2009 there have been several missions against Somali pirates or cross-border operations against the "Lord's Army," or attempts to apprehend jihadist commanders in their Somali lairs. The possibility of an SOF commitment is always present because their use depends more on the immediate mission than it does on general foreign policy goals.

The best illustration of the on-again, off-again use of SOF is surely in Iraq. There the original special operations took place in the Persian Gulf in the late 1980s and were about ensuring the safety of oil tankers transiting international waters. The SOF returned to Iraq and Kuwait in 1990–91 and helped fight a war—searching for enemy missiles, scouting, and helping liberate Kuwait City. After that war SOF remained in Kurdish Iraq to render humanitarian assistance to a starving tribal population. From 2003 to 2011 SOF were back in Iraq to fight another war, first against the Iraqi government, then a jihadist resistance. Leaving Iraq once more, the operators have returned in just the last year (2014)—again to Kurdistan (as well as other parts of the country)—to help stiffen local defenses against a new movement, the Islamic State of Iraq and the Levant (ISIL), a jihadist attempt to carve a "caliphate" out of portions of both Iraq and Syria. The facts that the Iraqi government itself had spurned a US residual force in that country, inviting the American withdrawal, and that the US government is in active opposition to the government of Syria—also an enemy of ISIL—show how remote from US foreign policy objectives an intervention can be. For the operators, however, the mission is the thing.

Are There Cost-Effectiveness Issues?

One argument favoring SOF in the past is that achieving a given (feasible) mission by unconventional means is a cheaper, better alternative than using conventional force. It is certainly true that USSOCOM represents a very small slice of overall US military spending, less than 2 percent in 2012. But these equations are subject to change. The most expensive items on SOCOM's shopping list today are aircraft and naval vessels. The long-range defense investment plan, reviewed every four years, is currently due for revision. The existing plan provides for 165 aircraft in the USSOCOM fleet. Of these the tilt-rotor V-22 "Osprey" and the new-generation MH-60M "Black Hawk" helicopter are midway through or beginning deployment. Both craft are expensive and a stealth version of the MH-60 even more so. But there are large SOCOM aircraft that are decades old, including both gunships and transports.

The Osprey merits special comment. This aircraft uses a novel tilt-rotor arrangement so that it can take off or land as a helicopter but fly like a plane, with considerable advantages in speed and range over a conventional chopper. The Osprey had a tumultuous design and production history. Much of that was due to the physical strain on equipment of engine mountings that change configuration and alter air flow. Dick Cheney canceled the program as too expensive back in the early 1990s, when he was secretary of defense for the first President Bush. Having first flown in 1989, it did not enter the forces until 2006. Originally planned for a development budget of $2.5 billion and an overall cost about ten times that, at current prices a smaller number of aircraft will be purchased for more than twice that amount. With air force special operations the V-22s only became active in 2009. Most Ospreys coming to the air force will go to SOCOM, and two squadrons have been activated so far. The air force expects to receive its final Osprey in 2015 or 2016. Aircraft readiness rates remain low and the estimated lifetime cost of the plane continues to rise. There are also hovering problems—dust when above a landing zone and heat damage to ship flight decks. Nevertheless the Osprey provides SOF a unique capability.

Among unique equipment that Special Operations Forces have adapted or designed from scratch are new kinds of light, all-terrain vehicles; communications devices; optics, including both day and nighttime scopes; and the stealth helicopter model revealed in the bin Laden raid. Air force special operations is experimenting with two types of foreign-manufactured light aircraft designed for rough terrain landings and easy maintenance. In 2009 the navy abandoned what it called the

Advanced SEAL Delivery System, which would have been a new-generation longer-range submersible. The defense investment plan that emerges from the next four-year policy review may well reason that reductions are necessary. The rhetoric of McRaven's SOCOM 2020 initiative seems to anticipate this. Time will tell.

It has been a historical strength of SOF that the unconventional warriors have taken standard military equipment and modified it. The forces have also commissioned equipment on their own. Sometimes that can be a problem. In an odd reprise of 1980s procurement scandals that befell Richard Marcinko and SEAL Team Six, the same unit is today under scrutiny for its purchases of equipment, in this case silencers for firearms that were intended to be untraceable. In the current case an auto mechanic, the brother of a senior navy intelligence planner, was hired to make 349 silencers, for which he charged $1.6 million in all, though they cost just $10,000 to make. Officers of the SEAL team told detectives of the Naval Criminal Investigative Service that they had never heard of the purchase. Navy officials destroyed documents that may have included whatever paperwork covered this deal, which actually traced to a directorate of the navy staff. This may turn out to be an innocent case of huge expenses for exotic gear, or it might actually be a scandal. After criminal investigation two cases resulting from this deal went to trial in federal court in October 2014.

Are There Predictable Social Issues on the Horizon?

Yes. The question of women is the most obvious—and is certainly an unresolved tension. For some years all the armed forces have been consumed with questions around integrating women into the military. In particular the opening to women of military specializations that involve combat has been a matter of controversy. Former Secretary of Defense Chuck Hagel has made January 2016 a deadline for all the armed services to integrate women. When questioned by Congress upon his nomination to lead SOCOM, Admiral McRaven said, about women in combat, that the Special Operations Command follows Pentagon policy. McRaven added that women were already attached to SOF for selected, gender-appropriate purposes (such as searching female suspects), and in some noncombat roles.

In the early 1980s, and again a decade later, the Delta Force experimented with including a few women in its intelligence cell called the "Funny Platoon." The idea at the time was to have the capacity to infiltrate agents into an operating area—much like the Intelligence Support Activity—with the ability to use a husband-and-wife cover story. These women were isolated within a supermacho world and they soon drifted off to other work. The need to deal with Muslim women in Iraq and Afghanistan brought out an urgent need for women. The first female students at the Kennedy Special Warfare School were trained to work with "cultural support teams" in the field and graduated from the Fort Bragg program in December 2010. When the women graduated, Army Special Forces commander Major General John Mulholland spoke at the commencement. "This is a landmark moment," Mulholland declared, "a significant step that is long overdue."

Precedent also favors inclusion of women. For decades the military resisted accepting gay men, using many of the same arguments that have been employed about women. Now gays serve with distinction and the threatened disruptive influence has been nil. A more serious problem will be abusive behavior toward women, but that is a phenomenon affecting all the armed forces, not merely SOF. Speaking of phenomena, we have the case of Senior Chief Christopher T. Beck, a decorated veteran of SEAL Team Six with seven combat deployments (Purple Heart, Bronze Star) and twenty years of service, who retired to change gender as Kristen Beck. The times they are a changin'.

As branches within armed services, Secretary Hagel's order does not directly impact SOF, only their parent services, but the trend is there. With its elite warrior corps, SOF resistance has been considerable. Yet across the board the tide is ebbing against women in combat, and at a certain point Special Operations Forces will be affected. Leaders are aware of that. Major General Bennet Sacolick, who headed the Kennedy School until 2012, has said that "We're looking for smart, qualified operators. There's a new dynamic. The days of 'Rambo' are over."[4] Sacolick was talking about men who can understand cultures, speak a foreign language, and work with indigenous populations, but that applies to women as well.

SOCOM has subsequently conducted opinion surveys on women Special Operations Forces troopers, and commissioned the Rand Corporation to study the social and behavioral effects of bringing women into SOF. Women have agitated to break the glass ceiling that has kept them out of combat roles, and as part of that, out of Special Forces. Male troopers will also need convincing that women can be effective operators. Still, it is a fair bet that there will be women SOF before the title year of Admiral McRaven's strategic concept comes up.

Do Other Countries Have Special Forces?

Apart from any other consideration, the competitive impulse makes it unlikely the United States would give up its Special Operations Forces. More than a hundred other nations maintain elite troops of this kind, starting with the United Kingdom, whose Special Air Service (SAS) in many ways served as the prototype for the American elite corps. American SOF, in turn, have formed and trained Special Forces in countries like Iraq and Afghanistan. Our European allies, to include France, Germany, Belgium, the Netherlands, Poland, the Baltic, and Eastern European states, all have equivalent military units. Israeli Special Forces, the Sayeret, are some of the most storied in the world. Australia and New Zealand have special warfare formations patterned on the British SAS. Lands that employ units of this kind range from historically neutral countries

(Switzerland, Sweden, Austria) to Latin friends challenged by drug traffickers (Mexico, Bolivia, Colombia, Peru, Chile), to African republics (Burkina Faso, Benin, Gabon, Cameroon). Russia has the dreaded *spetsnaz*, run directly by the Security Service, the Ministry of Defense, or separately attached to its military districts and the four fleets that still comprise the Russian navy. *Spetsnaz*, whether army or navy, are widely suspected of having had a hand in the 2014 separatist movements in the Crimea and the Ukraine. The Ukraine itself has several *spetsnaz* units under the military plus one that belongs to the Interior Ministry. In East Asia, China began to take an interest in SOF-type forces during the 1980s and began forming specialized units around the turn of the century. It now possesses an SOF Command within the People's Liberation Army, thought to total between 7,000 and 14,000 troops, plus at least two SOF-type battalions in its Marine Corps.

So You Want to Be an Operator?

"The Only Easy Day was Yesterday." So goes the SEAL motto, and it can be applied widely throughout Special Operations Forces. If it's worth doing, it's worth doing right, and—in terms of training—SOF spare no effort to get everything just right. You can be certain you'll face challenges on your road.

The marines select in-service. They do not recruit directly for MARSOC but want soldiers with five to ten years' experience. Except for second-tier logistics people (combat service support), all SOF marines, including direct support people, have to go through the selection. Screening begins with a review of the files, medical checks, physical fitness testing, qualification testing, and psychological evaluation. Next comes selection orientation, a three-week course in which candidates have the opportunity to recalibrate from their previous duty and improve fitness and skills for the actual assessment and selection. That is a nineteen-day ordeal of tests of every kind. Those who pass enter a four-phase individual training course.

The initial stage focuses on physical training and survival skills—candidates take the SERE (Survival, Escape, Resistance, and Evasion) program that has been much in the news of late because of the Bush administration's so-called enhanced interrogation techniques. The following two months are in-depth training on tactics and heavy weapons, with full-scale exercises built in. Only after passing these stages do the candidates spend five more weeks on communications, individual weapons, and close combat, with more exercises thrown in. After that comes seven weeks of training in unconventional warfare, with more field exercises. If you pass all of these things you graduate to *advanced* training. Most candidates do not make the cut, or do so after more than one try.

The other services—*and* the "Tier 1" special units like Delta and SEAL Team Six—have equally rigorous processes. Twice a year a team pores over military personnel records to find prospects and those soldiers are invited to stand for selection. When Chargin' Charlie Beckwith first created Delta Force, the Ranger/Special Forces physical training test for Rangers and Special Forces graded every trooper, regardless of age, by the same standard that would be applied to a seventeen-year-old. Since the unit was looking for mature soldiers, most candidates were five or ten years older than that. Pushups, sit-ups, run-dodge-jump, inverted crawl, and the two-mile run were only the beginning. There were land navigation tests, day and night for nearly three weeks. The Delta selection ends with the "Stress Phase." More than half the candidates wash out before that ever happens. A no-notice, middle-of-the-night call for a wilderness march over the Appalachian mountains with full pack, no map, and no stated objective or duration caps the challenge. In the late 1980s Delta trainers considered it exceptional if more than a dozen candidates passed out of a hundred who tried.

Army recruits can volunteer for Special Forces. There is a program called 18 X-Ray that sets a recruit up for airborne and Special Forces training after completing basic. Requirements include American citizenship, a high school degree (with at least a year of college preferred), high scores on the armed services vocational aptitude tests, sharp vision, a good checkup by service doctors, plus a high pass on the Army Physical Fitness Test, eligibility for a security clearance at the "secret" level, and a pass on swimming tests and a pretraining physical tasks list. But for Delta and for Green Beret officers, candidates are selected from within the service just like the marines. Army Special Forces reviews 500 personnel files of captain-rank officers each year and invites 350 to try out. General Reeder remarks the Green Berets need only about 150 captains, so they can afford to be selective. In 2012 the Special Forces actually admitted 107. If the SOF are reduced in upcoming military budgets, its staffing requirements will diminish and hence Special Forces qualification standards should be expected to increase.

The selection, called the "Q Course" (for "qualification") moves through stages depending upon the trainee's intended specialty and foreign language aptitude. Usually the first stage consumes at least a year, and it can take nearly two (fifty-five to ninety-five weeks) to impart essential skills. The Q Course builds up to an exercise long known as "Robin Sage," where the troops treat the western counties of North Carolina as a country, with guerrilla movements, prisoners to rescue, every kind of objective to test their mettle. (The Green Berets work out of a compound informally known back in the 1980s as "Rowe U"—or university—named for Green Beret Nick Rowe, whose story was famous from Vietnam days.) Only then do new troopers begin such advanced courses as the sniper, free-form parachutist, or combat diver programs. Green Berets then train as weapons, engineer, or communication specialists; intelligence operatives; or medics. At any given time there are several thousand men and women in some stage of training at the John F. Kennedy Special Warfare Center and School.

The SEALs build up to "Hell Week." They expect up to 90 percent of candidates to drop out. Those who make the selection face basic training—four phases covering fifteen months—then another year of individual and unit training. There is a Naval Special Warfare Prep School to start with. The cornerstone of the training program, as it has been since World War II, is underwater demolition. Today's descendent is a six-month course called BUD/s (Basic Underwater Demolition/SEAL). That is followed by the even longer SEAL Qualification Training program. The three-week parachute training course is almost a relief. Those elements simply prepare the candidate. As in the army's system, the navy prepares its fighters with extensive additional practice—six months for specialized skills, the same for unit training, then an equal interval for training at the task group level. A soldier or sailor's entire enlistment can be consumed moving through the stages of special operations training. No one should question the skills of SOF troopers who pass through these programs.

What about Fayetteville, North Carolina?

Some soldiers think of Fort Bragg as the most unremarkable of places, spread over the Sand Hills of North Carolina. The SEALs have gorgeous vistas at Coronado, on the Pacific Coast, and at least water at Little Creek, Virginia. Bragg had few distinctions. The original psychological warfare school and special warfare training center on "Smoke Bomb Hill" gives the flavor. When the Delta Force formed in the late 1970s, its initial compound was the old Fort Bragg stockade, or military prison. Later Delta moved to an out-of-the-way site at "Range 19," originally an artillery firing range, where in the mid-1980s the beige walls and red gabled roofs looked sort of like a Mediterranean coastal village. There are "Sicily" and "St. Mere Eglise Drop Zones" for practice parachute drops, and barracks, housing, and headquarters buildings in sections like Anzio Acres, Normandy Heights, or Corregidor Courts.

The base has always been tribal—and there are many tribes. Paratroopers of the Eighty-Second Division and Eighteenth

Airborne Corps have their favorite bars and hangouts. So do the Rangers of the Seventy-Fifth Regiment, the staff of the John F. Kennedy Special Warfare School and the Army Special Forces command, the Green Berets of the group in residence, and the operators of Delta. All those elites take a dimmer view of new arrivals—personnel of the army's reserve and readiness commands that relocated to Fort Bragg in base realignments a decade ago.

The town next to Fort Bragg, Fayetteville, is the sixth largest in North Carolina, with a population currently estimated at 209,000. It is in the Sand Hills on the western edge of Carolina's coastal plain, on the Cape Fear River. A classic southern town, during the 1950s there were racial divisions—blacks were rarely seen on High Street, the main drag, and those who lived off-base were mostly in the Spring Lake district. The cops concentrated their speed traps disproportionately there along Murchison Road. Blacks and whites even had different NCO clubs. That's gone now, but neighborhoods still reflect the old social divisions. African Americans account for almost exactly half the population, outnumbering whites (at 42 percent). And class has replaced race as the social fault line. Haymount and Van Story Hills are still nice, Murchison road still a backwater. The main routes into town join at a rotary around Market House. The town of Fayetteville has a bad rep. Among the nicknames for it are "Fayettenam" and "Fatalburg."

Payday at Fort Bragg makes the local shopkeepers ecstatic. Bragg and its associated Pope Air Force Base are the backbone of the local economy, accounting for $4.5 billion a year in regional spending. Fayetteville remains the quintessential American military town, its businesses ranging from chain eateries like McDonalds and Chilis, to the mega-commercial retailers of the Cross Creek Mall, to the narrow streets of the old town with their mom-and-pop shops. Home stores range from the local Holmes to the giant Lowe's. Walmart was the second-largest private employer in the town in 2010 (only exceeded by the healthcare system), but local outposts of major defense contractors have been moving in. Old textile mills have closed their doors. The largest concentration of employment is in retail services.

Tensions exist between military and civilians that are inherent in an army town, but the operators love it, as all the services' SOF people do their home ports and bases. This place, like the other "first to war" homes of our Special Forces community, is the culmination of a decades-long struggle to establish the need for a certain military capability, create that force, and then make space to house it. For the foreseeable future Special Operations Forces will remain at the cutting edge of American military power.

WHO'S WHO IN SPECIAL FORCES

Harry C. Aderholt (1920–2010). In effect the father of air force special operations, "Heinie" Aderholt was a pilot in an air transport unit in North Africa and Italy in World War II. Planes like his had been involved in so-called Carpetbagger flights, inserting and supporting intelligence missions and special operations. After the war the air commando units that had been the mainstay of aerial special operations were disbanded, so when the Korean War began the carpetbagger mission went to the Special Duty Detachment 2 of the Twenty-First Troop Carrier Squadron, which Aderholt led. His next assignments were to air intelligence service groups as the air force came to recognize the special operations mission. Aderholt's original unit continued to work with the CIA on covert operations in the Far East. In 1960 Aderholt returned to that region, where he was a major mover in air force adoption of the short-takeoff-and-landing Pilatus Porter aircraft. Aderholt himself designed and laid out a system of airfields in Laos called "Lima Sites" that enabled the United States to carry out special operations there. Colonel Aderholt then helped establish the First Air Commando Wing, recreating air force capability in this area. Back in Southeast Asia, he helped establish the "Bright Light" element of SOG and went to Thailand to form the Fifty-Sixth Air Commando Wing, which carried out low-altitude night missions against the Ho Chi Minh Trail. He served as operations chief for air force unconventional warfare and returned to Thailand in June 1970 as deputy in, and then chief of, the US military mission there. When communist Pathet Lao forces toppled the government of Laos in May 1975, Brigadier General Aderholt mounted an emergency evacuation of the CIA secret base at Long Tieng, which saved many Hmong warriors in Laos.

Aaron H. Bank (1903–2004). In 1943, a tactical training officer with a railroad battalion, Bank saw a notice that men with foreign language capabilities might be chosen for special assignments. He applied and ended up with the Office of Strategic Services. He parachuted into France with an OSS Jedburgh team and later was sent to Indochina. After the war, as a lieutenant colonel on General Robert McClure's staff, Bank became a proponent of the creation of Special Forces. He led the Tenth Special Forces Group, the first Green Beret unit. Bank set the standard for the Green Berets, and, at one point, wrote a memorandum requesting that they be allowed to wear berets, a proposal rejected at the time. Retiring as a colonel in 1957, Bank did not witness their emergence during the Vietnam era. If there is one individual to be given credit as the "father of the Green Berets," that would be Aaron Bank.

Charles Beckwith (1929–1994). Athletic enough to be recruited by the Green Bay Packers out of college, Beckwith joined the army instead. He was an early volunteer for Special Forces, where he earned the sobriquet "Chargin' Charlie." Beckwith led Detachment B-52, the original Project "Delta," in South Vietnam, with an important role in the 1965 battle of Plei Me. He led an airborne battalion on his second Vietnam tour. Beckwith went on, in 1977, to create the first Special Forces counterterrorism unit, First Special Forces Operational Detachment–Delta, which he led on

"Eagle Claw," the Iranian hostage rescue mission of 1980. He retired the following year as a full colonel.

Donald D. Blackburn (1916–2008). Commissioned in 1940, Blackburn was with a unit of the Philippine army when World War II began and the Japanese invaded. He and Russell Volckmann escaped Bataan and organized partisan resistance on the island of Luzon. After the war Blackburn worked at the Pentagon and NATO and was an instructor at West Point. He was an early military adviser in South Vietnam, heading there in 1957 to work with the South Vietnamese general commanding in the Mekong Delta. At Fort Bragg he then led the Seventh Special Forces Group. In that capacity Blackburn selected Bull Simons to lead the White Star force to Laos. Colonel Blackburn returned to Vietnam in 1965 to head MACSOG. He then functioned as deputy director for development of the deceptively named Defense Communications Planning Group, which aimed to seal the Demilitarized Zone between the Vietnams with an electronic barrier also known as the "McNamara Line." SOG teams were closely involved in placing sensors for that early version of the electronic battlefield. A lieutenant colonel at the end of the World War II, though not promoted for ten years afterward, Blackburn finally became an exception to the early rule that no one from the Special Forces community could attain flag rank. As a brigadier general he became the JCS special assistant for counterinsurgency and special activities, and in that role conceived and planned Operation Kingpin, the Sontay raid. General Blackburn retired in 1971.

William G. Boykin (1949–). Boykin entered the army through ROTC at Virginia Tech, and served in infantry, armor, and airborne units. He had a short tour with the 101st Airborne Division in Vietnam near the end of the war there. He came to SOF only in 1978, but went directly into the Delta Force. "Jerry" Boykin is probably the longest-serving

Delta Force soldier. Known for his fundamentalist religious views, Boykin was the operations officer under Charlie Beckwith at Desert One. Comrades remember him reciting prayers in a hanger in Egypt before Delta launched. With an interruption for the course at the Army War College, Boykin served continuously with the Delta Force until the mid-1990s, commanding the unit from 1992 to 1994, a time when some of Colonel Boykin's operators fought in the battle of Mogadishu, and others participated in the hunt for drug lord Pablo Escobar. Boykin went to Colombia for the Escobar operation and is rumored to have been in on the kill. As a brigadier general he then went to the CIA as a deputy in its paramilitary operations unit, the Special Activities Division. Boykin headed the army's Special Operations Command (1998–2000) and the John F. Kennedy Special Warfare Center (2000–2003), and served as deputy undersecretary for defense for intelligence, including special operations (2003–7). He retired as a lieutenant general after a controversy over the public articulation of views inappropriately characterizing enemies in the war on terror.

Lewis H. Burruss (c. 1942–). Born in Richmond, Virginia, to an Old Army father, "Bucky" Burruss majored in history and English in college. He enlisted in the army and graduated near the top of his OCS class, becoming a second lieutenant and immediately volunteering for Special Forces. Arriving in-country, a former CO recognized Burruss and pulled him into the Mike Forces, in which he fought for nearly two years. Before ever taking Infantry Officers' Advanced training, Burruss led the Second Mobile Strike Force Battalion in Vietnam. After several years with regular troops in Germany, Burruss returned to Fort Bragg as a Special Forces instructor. Charlie Beckwith selected Burruss as his second, and the two became the key figures in creation of the First Special Forces Operational Detachment–Delta (Delta Force). Bucky Burruss trained SFOD-D, put it through unit certification, was Beckwith's deputy commander at Desert One, and went to Grenada as the deputy SFOD-D commander during the "Urgent Fury" invasion as well as the *Achille Lauro* affair. Burruss was selected as mission commander for the abortive POW rescue mission into Laos in 1981, he was commended by the British Special Air Service for helping them during the 1982 Falklands war, and he participated in special missions in the Middle East and Central and South America. He retired from the army as a lieutenant colonel at the beginning of 1987.

Albert M. Calland III (1952–). "Bert" Calland hailed from Columbus, Ohio, far from the sea. Perhaps that was why he wanted to be a sailor. Just too young for the Vietnam War, Calland graduated from Annapolis in 1974 and immediately sought to become a SEAL. He passed the basic underwater demolition with Class 82, took his place with a SEAL underwater delivery platoon, and rose to lead both delivery and strike platoons. He has also been an instructor and an official dealing with research and development issues. In 1987, while Calland served as executive officer of Special Boat Team 12, he was sent to the Persian Gulf as part of the US effort to ensure freedom of navigation through those waters. Later he led the SEAL task unit in the Pacific. From 1992 through 1995 Captain Calland led SEAL Team One. For two years beginning in mid-1997 he commanded the superelite SEAL Team Six. Next he was selected to lead the special operations task force for CENTCOM. In that guise Rear Admiral Calland became the SOF supremo for the invasion of Afghanistan. In the summer of 2002 this SEAL officer moved up to head the entire Naval Special Warfare Command, and in the spring of 2004 he went to the CIA as associate director, then deputy director, for military support. His final government position would be as the top operational planner for the National Counterterrorism Center. Bert Calland retired as a vice admiral in 2007 and became an executive vice president with the think tank and military contractor CACI International Incorporated.

John T. Carney (1941–). Unlikely as it might seem, John Carney arrived at special operations through football. He played football for the University of Arizona, graduating in 1963 with an ROTC commission into the air force, where Carney essentially became the father of the SOF ground controller units called the Special Tactics Squadrons. Failing to qualify for flight training, Carney went to Vietnam as a "special services" officer, charged with organizing intramural sports and entertainment. In 1968 his old football coach at Arizona invited Carney to the Air Force Academy, where he was now coach and Carney would be his assistant—inviting the nickname "Coach Carney" that followed Carney throughout his career. Leaving the academy in 1974, Carney decided he would try his hand at "combat control," the kind of pathfinder role SOF needs for inserting airplanes into little-known places, and an air commando function that had fallen into such disregard that superiors did not even know what it was. Carney ended up practically creating the capability from whole cloth, and the first unit, near Charleston, was called simply "Brand X." Carney's combat controllers were keys to "Eagle Claw," the Iran hostage rescue, and it was Major Carney who accompanied a CIA air crew to the planned Desert One airbase site to install runway lights and test the weight-bearing properties of the desert there. With the Grenada invasion the preparation seemed so messed up to Carney that he retired, but the air force recalled him to active service after a few months and Coach successively created the 1723rd and 1724th Combat Control Squadrons, which became the 24th Special Tactics Squadron. Coach Carney's combat controllers had key roles in operations in Panama, the Persian Gulf, Kurdistan, Iraq, and Afghanistan. Coach Carney retired for a second time in 1991, and became a motive force in the Special Operations

Warrior Foundation, which provides scholarship money to the children of SOF soldiers fallen in the line of duty.

William O. Darby (1911–1945). Darby joined the artillery upon graduating West Point in 1933. He was a jack of all trades, leading cavalry and infantry detachments, as well as serving as a staff officer. Though placing only in the middle of his class at the Point, Darby was persuasive and often dominated conversations. That he did in June 1942, when, as aide to the general commanding the US Thirty-Fourth Infantry Division, Captain Darby was assigned to solicit volunteers from that and the First Armored Division to create an American version of the British commandos. Promoted major, Darby then led the First Ranger Battalion in the North African landings of November 1942, in Tunisia, and in Sicily. For the Anzio invasion of January 1944 Darby led an ad hoc Ranger regiment, then a regular infantry formation. He went to Washington briefly as a colonel on the War Department staff but returned to Italy escorting a survey team, only to be recruited as assistant commander of the Tenth Mountain Division. Near Lake Garda just two days before the end of the war Colonel Darby was fatally wounded by German artillery fire.

Roger H. Donlon (1934–). As a captain leading ODA-726 at Nam Dong in the Central Highlands of Vietnam, Donlon became the first Green Beret to win the Congressional Medal of Honor, when the camp was attacked on July 6, 1964. A New Yorker, Roger Donlon had actually first served in the air force, but was then appointed to West Point. He resigned from the Corps of Cadets but then enlisted in the army and gained a commission through Officer Candidate School. Donlon joined Special Forces in the summer of 1963 and South Vietnam would be his first duty post. The attack on Nam Dong by more than a battalion of the enemy took place a couple of months into the A-Team's assignment, at a point it had just completed installation of the fortifications protecting the village. Donlon became not only the first Green Beret but also the first American soldier of any branch or service to be awarded the nation's highest decoration in the Vietnam War. The heroic story of the defense of Nam Dong inspired many young Americans. Later Donlon directed infantry training for a US division in South Korea, and he returned to Vietnam for a second tour as an adviser in Kien Hoa province in 1972. Donlon retired in 1988 as a full colonel.

Wayne A. Downing (1940–2007). Graduating West Point in 1962, Downing, who would retire as a four-star general, took Ranger training but served in infantry and airborne billets for most of a decade, including two extended tours in Vietnam. He also served as an analyst with the Office of the Secretary of Defense. He arrived in Special Forces as a senior officer with the Seventy-Fifth Ranger Regiment in 1975, commanding its Second Battalion from 1977 to 1979, and the full regiment in 1984–85. For the next three years Downing was the deputy commander of the First Special Operations Command, and then director of USSOCOM's Washington office. As a major general Downing led the Joint Special Operations Command and its SOF Joint Special Operations Task Force in the Operation Just Cause invasion of Panama in 1989. He went on to command the army's own Special Operations Command (1991–93) and then USSOCOM (1993–96).

William E. Edge (1929–2003). A Floridian who joined the army out of high school and in time for the Korean War, Bill Edge was the renowned top enlisted man in Army Special Forces, ending his career as the command sergeant major of the John F. Kennedy Special Warfare School. Edge professed himself as influenced by newsreels of paratroopers in World War II and John Wayne war movies. He mustered out of the army when assigned to a "leg" infantry outfit after Korea, then promptly re-enlisted with the Eighty-Second Airborne Division. A boxer and Golden Gloves champion, a veteran of the First Cavalry Division in Korea, and a devotee of the board game Risk, Edge became a founder of the army's Golden Knights parachute display team, and is reputed to have coined that name, after the nickname for West Point's football team. Sergeant Edge made seven thousand parachute drops during his career. In Vietnam Sergeant Edge served with Fifth Special Forces Group and its Project B-57 Delta.

William F. Garrison (1944–). Perhaps because of their deep confidence in noncommissioned officers, or their own precarious rise within the army's hierarchy, the Special Forces have never been as difficult as other branches of the army about accepting officers who rose through the ranks. Bill Garrison is another example, commissioned through Officer Candidate School in 1966. He had started out as a private. Garrison served two tours in Vietnam, including service as an adviser with the program called "Phoenix" that aimed at eliminating the National Liberation Front infrastructure. He won the Purple Heart for wounds and the first of three Bronze Stars that would adorn his chest. In the early period of the Joint Special Operations Command, Garrison had a staff job there, and he went on to lead the Delta Force from 1985 to 1989. It was Bill Garrison's men who some say took out the drug lord Pablo Escobar. From 1992 to 1994 Garrison, as a major general, headed JSOC in his own right. In that capacity he led Task Force Ranger to Somalia and commanded it in the battle of Mogadishu. The "Black Hawk Down" battle sidetracked General Garrison's career, and he returned to head the John F. Kennedy Special Warfare School. He retired in 1996 after two years there, ironically on the same day his nemesis Mohamed Farah Aideed died in Somalia.

George W. Gaspard Jr. (1926–). Gaspard was a member of the very first Special Forces training class. He had been a marine in World War II, serving from 1944 to 1946, and came to the army as an officer in the summer of 1951. After initial training he volunteered for Ranger training and then applied to join the Tenth Special Forces Group. He became a team leader and soon was dispatched to Korea, where he served with the shadowy Far East Command–CIA 8240th Army Unit, running partisan operations into North Korea. Later he joined the Seventy-Seventh SFG, was an instructor, and then went airborne with the 187th Regimental Combat Team. Gaspard actually left the army in the late 1950s, but he held a Pentagon job early in the Kennedy administration and was then recalled to Special Forces. He held a succession of billets crucial to the war in the Central Highlands and along the DMZ, including helping to negotiate a truce between Montagnards in a quasi-rebellion with the South Vietnamese government, and returning on another tour to run SOG's scouts entering North Vietnam, the so-called STRATA Program. When one of the STRATA patrols got surrounded and needed emergency extraction, Major Gaspard went along too, personally descending through the jungle canopy to retrieve two of the trapped strikers. He retired as a Special Forces battalion commander and lieutenant colonel with First SFG in the summer of 1973.

Robert A. Gormly (1941–). Son of a ships' chandler, Bob Gormly worked two virtually full-time jobs (at J.C. Penney and Tastee-Freez) to pay his way through college. The routine, plus classes and extra math courses to graduate, make you wonder how he ever had time to see his girlfriend, much less go surfing, his favorite occupation. The fact that he did—and came up with the money to feel comfortable marrying—makes clear the reasons for Gormly's success. A surfer friend who was with a Navy Underwater Demolition Team (UDT) encouraged Gormly to try his luck as a sailor, and he joined the navy in 1963 and was commissioned through OCS. Gormly had some qualification problems due to an anomalous diving test, but he went on to be a combat swimmer who acquired a sterling reputation over a twenty-nine-year career. Gormly did two tours in South Vietnam's Mekong Delta with SEAL Team Two, leading a squad, then a platoon. He served as executive officer of UDT-22 and became the first battle veteran platoon leader to ever command SEAL Team Two. Gormly went on to lead UDT-12 and Naval Special Warfare Group 2. Gormly commanded SEAL Team Six in the "Urgent Fury" invasion of Grenada and the *Achille Lauro* affair, holding that position through 1986. He was then assigned as the top man for special warfare on the navy staff. He retired in 1992 as a captain.

Michael G. Healy (1926–). "Iron Mike" Healy led the Special Forces in Vietnam longer than any other officer. He also did no fewer than *five* tours of duty in the war. Healy's father was the chief of police in Chicago. The son, just too young for World War II, enlisted in the army in 1945 and was commissioned through OCS. He volunteered for airborne and for Ranger training. Lieutenant Healy led the Fourth Ranger Company, one of those Ranger units attached to combat divisions in the Korean War, winning the Bronze Star as well as his nickname. He held paratroop assignments and passed through a variety of training programs, as well as serving as the operations officer for the Tenth Special Forces Group in Germany. Healy's connection with Vietnam began in the summer of 1963 as senior US adviser to South Vietnamese Special Forces. He recruited and trained the first indigenous Mobile Strike ("Mike") Force battalion and happily endowed it with his own name. The next tour was as head of an airborne battalion, and Healy's third was as executive assistant to the senior US embassy official charged with pacification issues. He returned to Special Forces in a roundabout way. Colonel Healy came back to Vietnam in early 1969 as a staff officer and then an infantry brigade commander. He had just taken that formation home when General Creighton Abrams, who had dismissed the Fifth Special Forces Group commander over the "Green Beret Affair," asked Healy to come back. Colonel Healy led the Fifth Group for twenty months, though the spring of 1971—and General Abrams would ask him back again a year later to replace corps senior adviser John Paul Vann, tragically lost over the Central Highlands that were so familiar to Special Forces. Mike Healy led the Kennedy Special Warfare Center once he got back to the United States. He retired as a major general in 1981.

Gary L. Harrell (1952–). Big enough to play defensive tackle for East Tennessee State University, Gary Harrell was commissioned through ROTC in 1973. His baptism of fire came with the Eighty-Second Airborne Division in Grenada in 1983. He joined SOF after that. Harrell became a legendary operator. Bill Garrison, his former battalion CO, phoned Harrell one day to alert him the selection for SFOD-Delta was about to happen. Harrell, then with the Tenth Special Forces Group, went out for Delta and made it. In the Panama invasion Harrell went with the team that rescued American Kurt Muse from a Panamanian prison; he was in on the op against drug lord Pablo Escobar. Harrell led the Delta Force squadron and US raid in the battle of Mogadishu, October 3–4, 1993. In both Panama (from a helicopter crash) and Somalia (from an exploding mortar shell) Harrell was near death but cheated it. Colonel Harrell led the Delta Force in his own right from 1998 to 2000. During the 2001 US invasion of Afghanistan Brigadier General Harrell led the Special Operations Task Force under Central Command. He retired as a major general in 2008.

Francis J. Kelly (1920–1998). A Green Beret chief in Vietnam, Kelly was unusual in coming to Special Forces from the tank corps. Assigned to the Pentagon special warfare directorate in late 1963, he went out for airborne training and eventually took charge of the First Special Forces Group on Okinawa, where he became known as "Splash" for his agility in avoiding coral outcroppings during water parachute landings. The First Group became the foundation for Fifth SFG in South Vietnam, and which he led for a year starting in June 1966. Kelly created new entities to augment the combat power of the Fifth Group, including special boat units in the Mekong Delta and the Mike Force strike battalions, whose code name, "Blackjack," became his new nickname. Blackjack Kelly is author of the army's official monograph on Special Forces in Vietnam.

Joseph Robert Kerrey (1943–). A son of Nebraska, Kerrey was born there, was a businessman there, and served as its governor. Before that he joined the navy, passed the BUD/s course with Class 42, and served in Vietnam with SEAL Team One. As a lieutenant (junior grade) Kerrey led a SEAL platoon. A couple of months into his Vietnam tour, on March 14, 1969, Kerrey led a village raid in search of NLF cadre, which was acclaimed at the time but later became controversial. Lieutenant Kerrey suffered grave leg wounds from a grenade and was medically invalidated from the service. He went into politics and served for eighteen years in the US Senate. He has also been a university president, of the New School for Social Research in New York City.

Robert C. Kingston (1928–2007). General Kingston and Bob Kerrey have the University of Nebraska in common, though "Barbwire Bob" Kingston did the course there twenty years before. He joined the army as a private in 1948 and distinguished himself in the Korean War, where his unit was among those that reached closest to the Yalu River and the border of the People's Republic of China. His rifle platoon, lost with poor maps, picked up other drifting soldiers until it had more than a hundred men, whom Lieutenant Kingston was able to bring to safety. On a second Korea tour Captain Kingston became involved in unconventional warfare. On his return he instructed prospective Rangers at Fort Benning. As a Green Beret he was an early military adviser in South Vietnam, later commanded an infantry battalion, but took charge of the Third Special Forces Group in 1969. He returned to South Vietnam in 1972 as a brigadier general and deputy senior adviser for the Second Military Region, which he took over when his boss, John Paul Vann, died in a helicopter crash. Kingston moved on to Thailand in 1973 and helped create the unit that searched for Americans missing in action from the war. Barbwire Bob earned the Distinguished Service Cross and was twice awarded the Silver Star, among other medals. He commanded the Kennedy School from 1975 to 1977, when it had been relegated to an institution for military assistance, and was a sparkplug within army senior ranks pushing for the creation of the Delta Force. After leading an infantry division in South Korea, General Kingston became an early commander of the Rapid Deployment Joint Task Force, and he was the very first C-in-C of Central Command (CENTCOM). He retired as a full general in 1984, among those very few who serve in the army from private first class to four-star general.

James W. Kraus. An early Green Beret, Jim Kraus enlisted in the army in 1956 and joined Special Forces as soon as he became eligible. He numbered among the early US Special Forces advisers in South Vietnam, and served three tours in that war. Moving in and out of SOF posts, by 1990 Colonel Kraus was the commander of the Fifth Special Forces Group, responsible for the Middle East. His would be the major SOF command role in the Persian Gulf war.

Christopher Kyle (1974–2013). As a youngster in Texas oil country Chris Kyle couldn't decide whether he wanted more to be a cowboy or a military man. He made a try at ranching and rode broncos in rodeos, but then enlisted in the navy, where he became a SEAL in 1999, serving for a decade, with four combat deployments. Kyle specialized as a sniper, and his war was Iraq—where he said in a memoir, *American Sniper,* that the navy credited him with 160 kills and the enemy called him "the devil of Ramadi" and put a price on his head. After the military Kyle helped former soldiers with post-traumatic stress disorder and formed his own private security contractor firm, Craft International. Kyle and another man were murdered by a disturbed veteran at a Texas shooting range on February 2, 2013.

James H. Kyle. A thirty-year air force career for Colonel Kyle included a thousand crew flying hours in combat, most in Vietnam, and nine thousand flying hours in all. He was expert in the C 130 aircraft, with two thirds of his flights hours in that type, including gunship missions over the Ho Chi Minh Trail, and transport models flying into restricted bases, including into Ethiopia and South America. After Vietnam he led special operations for the Pacific Air Force command, capping a decade of SOF work. Afterward he took the USAF terrorism course at Hurlbut Air Force Base. Colonel Kyle was assigned to the logistics office for Kirtland Air Force Base when selected to lead the air force component of "Eagle Claw," the Iran hostage rescue. Kyle planned and organized the implantation of an instant air facility at the proposed Desert One site. Colonel Kyle would be the on-scene boss of the desert air "base."

Jeffrey R. MacDonald (1943–). Among Special Forces, Captain Jeffrey MacDonald became notorious for very different reasons—he was involved in the stabbing deaths of his wife and two children. A New Yorker, MacDonald attended good schools through Princeton University, and completed his medical internship at Columbia Presbyterian

Medical Center. He came to the army under the program that then financed medical studies in return for military service. In September 1969 MacDonald moved his family to Fort Bragg, where he had been assigned as senior doctor with Colonel Robert Kingston's Third Special Forces Group. On February 17, 1970, military police responded to an emergency at the MacDonald home and found the family dead. Captain MacDonald has always maintained he and his family were victims of a home invasion, but he was convicted of the murders in August 1979 and remains in prison at this writing.

Leroy J. Manor (1921–). Leroy Manor is the air force officer who led the joint task force that carried out the Sontay raid in November 1970. At that time Brigadier General Manor headed air force special operations. He was a veteran World War II fighter pilot with 72 combat missions in World War II and 275 in Vietnam, but he was a newcomer to unconventional warfare when he took over the Special Operations Forces. Manor's execution of the Sontay raid was nevertheless flawless. Manor retired as a lieutenant general and later served as a member of the Holloway Board, which reviewed the execution of the Iranian hostage rescue, Operation Eagle Claw.

Richard Marcinko (1940–). A SEAL notable for his Vietnam service, Marcinko became the first commander of SEAL Team Six and originator of the SEALs' "Red Team," responsible for testing the security of navy facilities, initially borrowing equipment from Team Six. In 1986 he became the target of a four-year-long investigation of improprieties in navy procurement for Red Cell through Team Six. Captain Marcinko's first trial ended in a hung jury, but he was convicted in 1990 and served time in federal prison for conspiracy to defraud the government.

Stanley A. McChrystal (1954–). As a young second lieutenant out of West Point, McChrystal became a paratrooper in the Eighty-Second Airborne Division. He passed the qualification tests for Special Forces in 1978, completing the course in April 1979 and leading an ODA in the Seventh Group. He then went on to infantry assignments and a stint with the United Nations security detachment at Panmunjom, Korea. McChrystal returned to the ranks of unconventional warriors in 1985, when he began an unusually long stint—more than three years—with the Third Battalion, Seventy-Fifth Ranger Regiment. Selected for the command and staff course at the Naval War College, he also earned a master's degree in international relations. He began alternating service duties with policy-oriented outside assignments, including as a fellow at Harvard's Kennedy School of Government and later with the Council on Foreign Relations. McChrystal had temporary duty with SOF in Saudi Arabia during the Gulf War of 1990–91, with his permanent assignment as a planner with the Joint Special Operations Command (JSOC). Following command of a paratroop battalion, he returned to SOF once more to lead the Second Battalion, Seventy-Firth Rangers, and later the full regiment. He was promoted to brigadier general in January 2001. McChrystal's service with the Eighteenth Airborne Corps is mentioned in the main text. After that his rise was meteoric, attaining the rank of lieutenant general early in 2006. He commanded JSOC from September 2003 until June 2008, a time during which SOF helped capture Saddam Hussein and led the mission that killed al-Qaeda in Iraq commander Abu Musab al-Zarqawi. His methods attained a notable integration of intelligence and SOF operations in Iraq. After a year directing the Joint Staff at the Pentagon McChrystal went to Afghanistan as a four-star general to lead the International Security Assistance Force and then all US troops there. He resigned that post and retired from the army in 2010 after publication of an article quoting officers very close to McChrystal as highly critical of President Barack Obama.

Robert A. McClure (1897–1957). A solid Midwesterner who played a formative role in the creation of Special Forces, Robert McClure was born in Illinois and commissioned from a private military college in Kentucky in time to serve through World War I. He had overseas duty in the Philippines and China and passed through the Army War College as early as 1935. When the United States entered World War II, McClure, a brigadier general, was the American military attaché in London. The army soon created an overseas headquarters for its forces in the European theater and assigned McClure to a senior position as chief of intelligence and psychological warfare. General McClure became the apostle for psychological warfare, convincing General Dwight D. Eisenhower of the value of these operations. Special Forces were originally conceived as an adjunct to the psychological warfare effort, in which McClure continued to play a key part postwar. He headed the Psychological Warfare Division on the army staff from 1950 through 1953, and the US military mission to Iran. He retired in 1956 as a major general.

William H. McRaven (1955–). A journalism major at the University of Texas, McRaven wanted to be a Green Beret after reading Robin Moore's book *The Green Berets*. His sister's boyfriend, a Special Forces man, told him he'd be better as a SEAL. He credits the Green Berets with sending him to the SEALs. He was commissioned from NROTC in 1977 and first served in the underwater demolition teams. As a young lieutenant and unit leader McRaven became a plank holder with SEAL Team Six. He later did tours with swimmer delivery units and Teams Four, One, and Three, commanding the latter in 1994–96. McRaven emulated Robin Moore's literary exploits, converting his Naval

Postgraduate School thesis into the book *Spec Ops: Case Studies in Special Operations Warfare, Theory and Practice* (1995), which has become a standard text in the field. He participated in Desert Storm as an operations planner with the Naval Special Warfare Command and held several other staff positions, including at the White House with the National Security Council staff from 2001 to 2003. He made rear admiral in 2004 while the operations chief for USSOCOM. Admiral McRaven then led all American SOF in Europe, and after that JSOC, where he planned and executed the bin Laden raid, narrated here in the prologue. He was promoted to full admiral afterward, in command of USSOCOM.

Richard J. Meadows (1932–1995). Lying about his age, Meadows enlisted as a paratrooper when fifteen years old. In Korea his unit defended against the initial Chinese intervention forces. He joined Special Forces in 1953 and went with the Tenth Special Forces when it deployed to Germany. Fearing his deception might be uncovered, Meadows rejected repeated offers to attend Officer Candidate School. In 1960 Meadows would be the first Green Beret NCO selected for a one-year tour of duty with the British Special Air Services regiment. His Southeast Asia adventures began in 1961 with assignment to the "White Star" project in Laos. Subsequently he served with the Eighth Group in Panama. He returned to Southeast Asia in 1965 and joined SOG, where he led RT Iowa and held the record for enemy captured, including some inside North Vietnam. General William Westmoreland gave Meadows a field promotion to officer's rank. In the 1970 Sontay raid Meadows would be a key leader, along with Bud Sydnor and Bull Simons. He then served as a Ranger and retired as a major in 1977. But Meadows was brought back as a civilian consultant on the creation of the Delta Force, and, in the Iranian hostage rescue, he made the on-scene preparations in Tehran for the Iran Hostage rescue.

Frank D. Merrill (1903–1955). An unusual character, Frank Merrill was one of the few army enlisted men to win entry into the US Military Academy. An engineer sergeant in Panama when he got the appointment to West Point, Merrill not only graduated from there, he went on to obtain a degree from MIT, and he served in Tokyo as a military attaché and Japanese language student. A cavalryman, promoted to major shortly before World War II, Merrill was assigned to Douglas MacArthur's staff but would be caught in Rangoon, Burma, when Pearl Harbor was attacked. He stayed on as a liaison to the British, and a staffer for General Joseph Stillwell, the senior US commander of the China-Burma-India (CBI) Command. In late 1943 Merrill was promoted to brigadier general and given charge of the 5307th Composite Unit (Provisional), code-named "Galahad" and soon known as Merrill's Marauders. He suffered a severe heart attack while leading his Rangers against the Japanese in March 1944, and another in May. He finished the war as chief of staff to Stillwell, by that time on Okinawa commanding the Tenth Army.

Ola L. Mize (1931–2014). Dropping out of high school to enlist in the army, Mize was rejected for being too small, but he succeeded after repeated attempts. After a tour with the Eighty-Second Airborne Division, Sergeant Mize went to Korea with the Third Infantry Division and, near the end of the war, won the Medal of Honor for an outnumbered fight against Chinese troops. He joined Special Forces and was commissioned from the ranks. By 1965 he was a Green Beret trainer, where he is credited with starting the combat divers qualification course at Key West. Mize served three tours in Vietnam with the Fifth Special Forces, leading A-, B-, and C-detachments, including the Mike Force known as the Third Mobile Strike Force Command, at the head of which he won the Silver Star. He retired as a colonel in 1981 after heading the John F. Kennedy Special Warfare Center.

Melvin Morris (1942–). A young African American from Oklahoma who believed that being in the army was better than being in trouble, Morris enlisted in the National Guard, moved to the active army, and joined Special Forces in 1961. He served two tours in Vietnam, the second as a company commander with the Fourth Mobile Strike Force Command in the Mekong Delta. There, as a sergeant in the fall of 1969, he led his Mike Force strikers to rescue another American, brought him back despite being wounded three times, and used grenades to destroy enemy bunkers that were pinning down the Mike Force. Sergeant Morris received the Bronze Star for this action, but in 2014 he was awarded the Medal of Honor.

James R. Paschall. An energetic and accomplished officer, "Rod" Paschall was Special Forces through and through, serving no fewer than five tours in Southeast Asia. He also accomplished the unusual feat, for an army officer, of graduating from the Naval War College, not just West Point. He was a team commander (A-2) with Montagnards in the Central Highlands as early as 1962. Paschall served in Laos during 1964, in South Vietnam again in 1966–68, and in Cambodia in 1974–75. In between combat tours he earned graduate degrees in international affairs and American history. The intellectual bent showed: at one point Paschall developed and promulgated an army counterinsurgency doctrine; at another he headed the Military History Institute at Carlisle Barracks, a premier center for research on army history. He wrote four books, including an oral history of the Korean War, a study of Germany at the end of World War I, and policy-oriented treatises on that Special Forces bugbear low-intensity conflict. Paschall edited a popular military history journal too. In the middle of all this, Colonel Paschall followed Charlie Beckwith in command of First Special Forces Operational Detachment–Delta. It was in fact Paschall who led the unit during the still-mysterious 1981 project for a Delta Force prisoner rescue in Laos that was short-circuited by the Bo Gritz affair.

Robert B. Rheault (1925–2013). From a prominent Boston family, Rheault graduated from prep schools and West Point (1946) and did work at the Sorbonne. He joined Special Forces in 1960. His assignments included missions to West Germany, Tunisia, Jordan, Iran, Pakistan, and the Himalayas during Sino-Indian war. His first Vietnam tour was in 1964; he then served with the Pentagon unit that supervised counterinsurgency and special activities. He returned to South Vietnam in 1969 as commander of Fifth Special Forces Group. Colonel Rheault had poor relations with US Vietnam chief General Creighton V. Abrams, which led to a blowup when Fifth Group personnel killed a local informant in the "Green Beret Affair." Rheault retired from the army in October 1969. He is said to be the model for the character Colonel Kurtz (Marlon Brando) in the Hollywood movie *Apocalypse Now*.

Jose Rodela (1937–). Leading a company of the Third Mobile Strike Force Command in a firefight in Phuoc Long province early in September 1969, Sergeant Rodela deployed his men under fire to break up a North Vietnamese attack, rescued comrades though wounded himself, and destroyed an enemy rocket position in a solo assault. At the time he received the Distinguished Service Cross for his efforts. In 2014 Sergeant Rodela was awarded the Medal of Honor for his feats.

James Nicolas Rowe (1938–1989). A Texan who nurtured dreams of being in the army, "Nick" Rowe won an appointment to West Point and graduated in 1960. In the Kennedy-era expansion of Special Forces Rowe became a Green Beret and went to South Vietnam in 1963 as deputy commander of Detachment A-23 at Tan Phu in the Mekong Delta. On October 29 First Lieutenant Rowe, his team leader, and another Green

Beret accompanied their South Vietnamese irregular unit on a sweep operation. They detected enemy guerrillas and pursued, only to be caught in an ambush. Lieutenant Rowe and both his comrades were captured. Rowe spent five years in an enemy prison camp, defiant to the end, and kept in a cage most of the time. He believed he had been slated to be executed when, on New Year's Eve in 1968, a US airstrike scattered the guards accompanying him, leaving just one to overpower. Rowe ran—and was seen by two UH-1 helicopters of the First Cavalry Division (Airmobile), one of which landed to rescue him. Rowe discovered he had been promoted to major while in captivity. He later married and authored a book on his experiences. Rowe retired in 1974, but the army recalled him seven years later as a lieutenant colonel and asked him to design a training course based on his POW years. It was Nick Rowe who created the Survival, Evasion, Resistance, and Escape (SERE) course that remains a requirement for US Special Forces, SEALs, marine operators, pilots, and other personnel even today. Colonel Rowe went on to serve with the US military advisory mission in the Philippines, where he was assassinated by communist insurgents on the morning of April 21, 1989. A key Special Forces training compound in North Carolina is named in his honor.

Clyde R. Russell. A paratrooper of the Eighty-Second Airborne Division, Clyde Russell parachuted into St. Mere Eglise, Normandy, on D-Day, with the same battalion whose commander was portrayed by John Wayne in the movie *The Longest Day*. In Korea Russell was an infantry officer in the Inchon invasion. He transferred to Special Forces in the late 1950s as executive officer of the Tenth Group in Germany. He led the Latin America–specialized Seventh SFG in 1962, at the time of the Cuban Missile Crisis. Then he volunteered for Vietnam. Colonel Russell became the first leader of the Studies and Observation Group (SOG). Russell retired from the army as a full colonel in 1968.

Barry Sadler (1940–1989). Born in New Mexico, Sadler grew up in Colorado, where he dropped out of high school to join the air force in 1957. He served one enlistment, as a radar operator in Japan, before switching to the army, where he completed airborne training and made the selection for Special Forces, then in their Kennedy-era expansion. Sadler rose to sergeant first class and became a medic. Sent to South Vietnam, Sadler was on patrol from a post near Pleiku in the Central Highlands in May 1965 when he was badly wounded in the knee by a guerrilla booby trap. Not realizing the wound was infected, Sergeant Sadler continued the mission, but later came near to death. He had to be evacuated to Walter Reed Hospital in Washington. In convalescence Sadler wrote his song "The Ballad of the Green Berets," which became a number one hit in the United States in the spring of 1966. He took to writing novels. A dozen years later the former Green Beret, in a dispute over a girlfriend, killed a Mississippi man, for which Sadler was convicted of voluntary manslaughter in 1979. On appeal Sadler's sentence was reduced to time served because of the dead man's threatening behavior before their confrontation. Barry Sadler relocated to Guatemala City in Central America, where in the fall of 1988 he was shot in the head by an unknown assailant while riding in a taxicab. Sadler had the unfortunate distinction of being returned to the United States for medical treatment for the second time in his life. He lay in a coma for several months, suffered brain damage, and died at his mother's home a little over a year after the Guatemala City shooting.

Peter J. Schoomaker (1946–). Like his compatriot Hugh Shelton, Peter Schoomaker rose to four-star general and attained a senior position in the US high command. A college football star at the University of Wyoming, Schoomaker was commissioned from ROTC and began his service as an infantry and armor officer. Schoomaker's career has been exceptional in several ways. First is his rapid rise, and his transition into SOF, where almost immediately Charlie Beckwith put him in command of a squadron of the Delta Force, which he led during the Iranian hostage rescue, "Eagle Claw." Following study at the command and general staff school Schoomaker went to an armored cavalry unit again, but returned to Special Forces as the chief operations planner for JSOC, then again commanded a squadron of the Delta Force (1985–88). Schoomaker was selected for the course at the National War College, then led the entire Delta Force (1989–92), after which he became assistant commander of the First Cavalry Division. This cycle of alternation between SOF and conventional forces is another unusual aspect of his career. From 1994 to 1996 General Schoomaker led JSOC, then the army's Special Operations Command, then USSOCOM (1997–2000). At that point he retired and became a business executive. But in 2003 Schoomaker was recalled to active service to become chief of staff of the US Army, the post he held until 2007. Schoomaker is not only the first SOF officer to head the US Army, he is the only officer ever to be recalled from retirement to serve in that position.

Henry Hugh Shelton (1942–). Henry Shelton obtained his commission through the Reserve Officers Training Corps and, though he began as an infantry officer, went through Ranger training, then Special Forces, and served in South Vietnam in 1966–67 with the original Delta Force (Fifth Group Project B-52), then at Ha Thanh village in command of ODA-104. Shelton returned to infantry and airborne assignments and was the assistant commander of the 101st Airborne Division in Operation Desert Storm. General Shelton went on to lead the Eighteenth Airborne Corps, then the US Special Operations Command, a post he held in 1996–97, immediately before rising to chairman of the Joint Chiefs of Staff (1997–2001). General Shelton was the first SOF officer ever to lead the US armed forces.

Arthur D. Simons (1918–1979). A reservist officer early in World War II, "Bull" Simons was with one of the last army artillery units to use pack mules. The Ninety-Eighth Artillery went to New Guinea, where it fought under General Douglas MacArthur. Simons's battery was incorporated into the Sixth Ranger Battalion, which gave him his first unconventional warfare experience. Simons did well, commanding a Ranger company and later as the battalion executive officer in the Philippines in 1944–45. He participated in the famous raid to Cabanatuan that freed inmates of the prison camp there and for which he won the Silver Star. Bull left the army as a major, but in 1951 the army recalled him to train Rangers. After a tour as a military adviser in Turkey he joined Special Forces' Seventy-Seventh Group. In 1960 he was chief of staff of the Army Special Warfare Center. A year later Lieutenant Colonel Simons led Project White Star troops in Laos, then served in Panama with the Eighth Special Forces Group. He went to Vietnam in 1965 assigned to SOG. Simons was chief of staff of the Eighteenth Airborne Corps when selected to lead the ground assault element in the Sontay raid. Simons retired in 1971 and formed a private security company, notably engaging in a daring rescue of two American business executives in Tehran after the Iranian revolution of 1979. He died soon afterward of a heart attack.

John K. Singlaub (1921–). An officer who never lacked for the courage of his convictions, Singlaub would be forthright to the end, wrecking his career in 1977 when, as chief of staff of the United States command in South Korea, he went public to dispute Carter administration plans to withdraw most remaining American troops from that country. Born in California, "Jack" Singlaub joined the army out of UCLA in 1943 and was seconded to the Office of Strategic Services (OSS). There he instantly became involved in special missions, including the OSS-British "Jedburgh" Program (he was with Team "James"), a foray at the time of the Japanese surrender to liberate Allied prisoners held in a camp on Hainan Island in China, and an expedition to survey conditions in French Indochina. Many army officers served with the CIA during the postwar years, and Singlaub did too, employed as an observer of the Chinese civil war in Manchuria. A Chinese communist tribunal pronounced a death sentence against him. In the Korean War he led the CIA-military covert operations unit called "JACK" (Joint Army-CIA Korea), a play on his own nickname. Toward the end of the war he led the Second Battalion of the Fifteenth Infantry Regiment, which would be his favorite career experience. Becoming a Green Beret, attending and instructing at army schools, and Pentagon duty kept Colonel Singlaub busy until 1966, when he was sent to South Vietnam to lead MACSOG, which he did for two years—his next-favorite military billet. He was promoted brigadier general in 1968 and retired as a major general. Jack Singlaub liked to crack that fighting communism was not a spectator sport, and he went on to play roles in right-wing organizations like the World Anti-Communist League. As an arms dealer he also became mixed up in the notorious Iran-Contra Affair, selling weapons to Nicaraguan anti-communist rebels for money they obtained through a US government conspiracy.

Carl W. Stiner (1936–). A product of Army ROTC from Tennessee Polytechnic Institute in his home state, Carl Stiner served as an infantry trainer before heeding President Kennedy's call to the Green Berets. He joined the Third Special Forces Group in 1964. Several years later, upon finishing the course at the army's Command and General Staff School, Stiner went to Vietnam but not as a Green Beret. Rather he served with the Fourth Infantry Division in the Central Highlands, where he was wounded. Rising in the ranks as a paratrooper, Stiner accumulated some interesting international assignments, including in Beirut at the height of the troubles there, in Saudi Arabia, and in the *Achille Lauro* affair. He was an early chief of staff of the Carter-era Rapid Deployment Joint Task Force, a predecessor to CENTCOM, and headed the Joint Special Operations Command, August 1984–January 1987, and the Eighteenth Airborne Corps, in which capacity Stiner would be the senior commander of the 1989 US invasion of Panama. He led the US Special Operations Command from June 1990 to May 1993. General Stiner is a member of the Ranger Hall of Fame.

Elliott P. ("Bud") Sydnor (1927–). Bud Sydnor actually shipped out as a sailor, a submariner no less, and spent the first years of the Cold War aboard the *Raton* in the Atlantic. But he went to a college that had only an Army ROTC program and graduated in 1952 as a young second lieutenant. Sydnor served with infantry and paratroop units and joined Special Forces in 1959. He was the first Green Beret officer selected for a year of exchange service with the British Special Air Services regiment. In 1961–62 Sydnor went to Laos with "White Star" and remained with Seventh Special Forces at Fort Bragg until 1964. His next Vietnam tour, in 1967–68, was with the paratroops. But while assigned to the army's infantry school at Fort Benning, in 1970 Bud Sydnor was tapped to lead the ground strike team for the Sontay raid, for which he received the Distinguished Service Cross. He later commanded the First Special Forces Group on Okinawa. Sydnor retired as a colonel in 1981.

James B. Vaught (1926–2013). A man who claimed he was a direct descendent of Francis Marion, the Revolutionary War "Swamp Fox," Vaught was commissioned from The Citadel in 1946. He served with the US Army in its occupation of Germany and led an infantry company in the Korean War. His first Vietnam tour came in 1967–68 as commander of the Fifth Battalion, Seventh Cavalry of the First Cavalry Division (Airmobile). In that command he played roles in the liberation of Hue after the Tet Offensive, and in Operation

Pegasus, which relieved the Marine combat base at Khe Sanh. He did a second Vietnam tour in 1971. Later Vaught led the Twenty-Fourth Infantry Division. He held a Pentagon job in 1979 when tapped to lead the Iranian hostage rescue mission. In the wake of its failure Vaught became an advocate for a permanent interservice special operations command. He retired in 1983 as a lieutenant general and commander of US forces in Korea. General Vaught was a conventionally trained officer who appreciated SOF and became an advocate for them.

Russell W. Volckmann (1911–1982). A 1934 graduate of West Point, Volckmann had wanted duty in the Philippines but had been relegated to various army posts in the United States. He did achieve his desire a year before Pearl Harbor and was in the Philippines when the Japanese invaded the islands at the end of 1941. Volckmann and Donald Blackburn became partisan leaders of troops who evaded the Japanese when they conquered the islands, and that experience formed the foundation for his advocacy of unconventional warfare methods. By war's end Volckmann was a colonel and had fought in the bush and organized a resistance force of 15,000 fighters. Afterward Volckmann became a key figure in compilation of the first army counterinsurgency manuals and an advocate for Special Forces on General Robert McClure's staff.

Lewis H. Williams (1926–). Like many Americans, "Mike" Williams enlisted to fight in World War II. He served with the Eighty-Eighth Infantry Division in Italy. Williams decided to make a career of it. Commissioned from Officer Candidate School in 1948, he was considered a go-getter, among the first volunteers for the Tenth Special Forces Group when the Green Berets were first created. In 1953 Williams went to Korea, where he led one of the shadowy Army/CIA irregular units, the Seventh Battalion, Third Partisan Regiment. He returned to Fort Bragg with the Seventy-Seventh Special Forces Group and later served with the 101st Airborne Division. Captain Williams left the army in 1960. Bored with civilian life, in 1964 Williams joined a mercenary unit with the Congolese army, Major Mike Hoare's 5 Commando, which had a key role in suppressing the Matabele rebellion and freeing Western hostages held in Stanleyville. A decade later Williams tried to enlist as a mercenary with UNITA rebels in neighboring Angola, but instead accepted a commission in the Rhodesian army, fighting a black nationalist revolution. Williams rose to major and commanded a squadron of a famed Rhodesian mounted unit, Grey's Scouts. He then worked as military affairs editor for *Soldier of Fortune* magazine. The journalist Robin Moore, partial to Green Berets and also to Rhodesia, teamed up with Williams to tell his story in the 1980 book *Major Mike*. During the 1980s Williams worked for a short time in El Salvador as a counterinsurgency adviser to its government.

Sherman H. Williford. A "soldier's soldier," Williford enlisted in the late 1950s and jumped at the chance to become a paratrooper. In 1960 he became a member of the original army parachute exhibition team called the "Golden Knights." Williford also stood up for Ranger training and obtained his commission from Officer Candidate School in 1964. He went to Vietnam and returned for a second tour as a rifle company commander in 1969. Selected early for the Command and General Staff School, Williford explored leadership concepts for his thesis. A rising star among Green Berets, he succeeded Rod Paschall in command of the Delta Force, which he commanded until 1985, including during the Grenada invasion. Williford retired as a brigadier general.

William P. Yarborough (1912–2005). A West Point classmate of Creighton V. Abrams, Bill Yarborough did a great deal to create the force at which Abrams would look askance when he led the Americans in Vietnam. After graduating in 1936 the young Lieutenant Yarborough would serve with the Philippine Scouts and missed being trapped there by World War II by a year when reassigned to the infantry demonstration regiment at Fort Benning. Yarborough was an early volunteer for the US paratroops and designed the boot, uniform, and emblem devices that would be used by US paratroops. He fought in North Africa and Sicily, relieved there as a parachute battalion commander, but redeemed himself at the Anzio invasion, where Yarborough led the 509th Parachute Battalion into battle alongside Darby's Rangers. Later in 1944 his airborne command, expanded, spearheaded Allied landings in southern France. Yarborough had security and intelligence assignments in the Four Powers occupation of Austria, a job he reprised in the late 1950s when he led the Sixty-Sixth Counterintelligence Group in Germany. He also headed the US military advisory group in Cambodia. In January 1961 Yarborough was named to head the Special Warfare School at Fort Bragg, where, as related, he proved a central figure in the rapid expansion of Special Forces—and their adoption of the Green Beret. In 1965 he went to Korea as a US member of the United Nations Military Armistice Commission, then returned to the Pentagon as top staff officer for Special Forces and psychological warfare. As a major general Yarborough headed army intelligence (G-2) from December 1966 through July 1968. His last active-duty assignment was as a corps commander in South Korea. William Yarborough retired as a lieutenant general in 1971.

Fred W. Zabitosky (1942–1996). "Zab" Zabitosky loved the army, which gave him the discipline and pride he had lacked. It turned him away from the life of petty crime he had embarked upon—complete with time in juvenile prison in Trenton, New Jersey, and gave him the structure that changed his life. Zabitosky joined the army in 1959, was given basic training at Fort Benning, and soon volunteered for Special Forces. By September 1967, when Sergeant First Class Zabitosky joined SOG's Reconnaissance Team Maine, he was on his third Vietnam tour. RT Maine made scout patrols, evaluated the damage from Arc Light strikes, and performed Bright Light rescue missions from the Central Highlands base of Kontum. On one of these missions on February 18, 1968, the team landed in the middle of an enemy base. Zabitosky took over from his team leader and led the SOG strikers to a succession of landing zones in an effort to find one safe enough to evacuate from. He saved two crewmen from a chopper that was burned out while trying to recover the RT. Sergeant Zabitosky received the Congressional Medal of Honor.

NOTES

Chapter 2

1. Quoted from "Green Berets," John F. Kennedy Presidential Library and Museum, http://jfklibrary.org/JFK/JFK-in-History/Green-Berets.aspx?view=print (retrieved January 4, 2014).

2. US Army, *Special Warfare, U.S. Army: An Army Specialty* (Washington, DC: Government Printing Office, 1962), 5.

3. John L. Plaster, *SOG: The Secret Wars of America's Commandos in Vietnam* (New York: Penguin Onyx, 1998), 355.

4. William H. McRaven, *Spec Ops: Case Studies in Special Operations Warfare. Theory and Practice* (New York: Ballantine Books, 1996), 318.

Chapter 3

1. Stanley McChrystal, *My Share of the Task: A Memoir* (New York: Penguin Books, 2013), 45.

Chapter 4

1. Department of Defense (Caspar Weinberger), *Annual Report to the Congress on the Fiscal Year 1985 Budget, Fiscal Year 1986 Authorization Request, and Fiscal Years 1985–1989 Defense Programs* (Washington, DC: Government Printing Office, 1984), 276.

Chapter 6

1. White House, "Remarks by the President at the United States Military Academy Commencement Ceremony," May 28, 2014 (http://www.whitehouse.gov/ the-press-office/ 2014/05/28/ remarks-president-united-states- military-academy- commencement- ceremony).

2. US Special Operations Command, "SOCOM 2020: Forging the Tip of the Spear," no date (c. 2012), 6.

3. US Special Operations Command, "Posture States of Admiral William H. McRaven before the 112th Congress Senate Armed Services Committee," March 6, 2012, 12.

4. Quoted in Paul D. Shinkman, "Special Ops Chief on Women in Combat: 'The Days of Rambo Are Over'," *U.S. News & World Report*, June 18, 2013, http://www.usnews.com/news/articles/2013/06/18/special-ops-chief-on-women-in-combat-the-days-of-rambo-are-over.

BIBLIOGRAPHY

Adams, Thomas K. *US Special Operations Forces in Action: The Challenge of Unconventional Warfare.* London: Franklin Cass, 1998.

Bahmanyar, Mir. *Shadow Warriors: A History of the U.S. Army Rangers.* Botley, UK: Osprey Press, 2005.

Bank, Aaron. *From OSS to Green Berets: The Birth of Special Forces.* Novato, CA: Presidio Press, 1986.

Barnett, Frank R., B. Hugh Tovar, and Richard H. Shultz, eds. *Special Operations in U.S. Strategy.* Washington, DC: National Defense University Press, 1984.

Bergen, Peter L. *Man Hunt: The Ten Year Search for Bin Laden from 9/11 to Abbottabad.* New York: Crown Publishers, 2012.

Berntsen, Gary, with Ralph Pezzullo. *Jawbreaker: The Attack on Bin Laden and Al-Qaeda: A Personal Account by the CIA's Key Field Commander.* New York: Crown Publishers, 2005.

Blaber, Pete. *The Mission, the Men, and Me: Lessons from a Former Delta Force Commander.* New York: Berkley Caliber, 2008.

Black, Robert W. *Rangers in Korea.* New York: Ballantine Books, 1989.

———. *Rangers in World War II.* New York: Ballantine Books, 1992.

Bowden, Mark. *Black Hawk Down: A Story of Modern War.* New York: NAL Signet, 2001.

Burruss, L. H. *Mike Force.* New York: Author's Guild, 2000.

Carney, John T., Jr., and Benjamin F. Schemmer. *No Room for Error: The Covert Operations of America's Special Tactics Units from Iran to Afghanistan.* New York: Ballantine Books, 2002.

Cawthorne, Nigel. *Warrior Elite: 31 Heroic Special Ops Missions.* Berkeley, CA: Ulysses Press, 2011.

Chalker, Dennis, with Kevin Dockery. *One Perfect Op: Navy SEAL Special Warfare Teams.* New York: Avon Books, 2002.

Clancy, Tom, with Carl Stiner. *Shadow Warriors: Inside the Special Forces.* New York: G. P. Putnam's Sons, 1988.

Conboy, Kenneth, and Dale Andradé. *Spies and Commandos: How America Lost the Secret War in North Vietnam.* Lawrence: University of Kansas Press, 2000.

Crumpton, Henry A. *The Art of Intelligence: Lessons from a Lifetime in the CIA's Clandestine Service.* New York: Penguin, 2012.

Dockery, Kevin. *Navy SEALs: The Complete History.* New York: Berkley Publishing, 2004.

———. *Navy SEALs II: The Vietnam Years.* New York: Berkley Trade, 2003.

———. *Operation Thunderhead: The True Story of Vietnam's Final POW Rescue Mission—and the Last Navy SEAL Killed in Country.* New York: Berkley Trade, 2009.

Durant, Michael J., and Steven Hartov, with Robert L. Johnson. *The Night Stalkers: Top Secret Missions of the U.S. Army's Special Operations Aviation Regiment.* New York: NAL Caliber, 2008.

Eversman, Matt, and Dan Schilling, eds. *The Battle of Mogadishu: Firsthand Accounts from the Men of Task Force Ranger.* New York: Ballantine Books, 2006.

Franks, Tommy, with Malcolm McConnell. *American Soldier.* New York: Regan Books, 2004.

Fury, Dalton (pseud.). *Kill Bin Laden: A Delta Force Commander's Account of the Hunt for the World's Most Wanted Man.* New York: St. Martin's Press, 2008.

Geraghty, Tony. *Black Ops: The Rise of Special Forces in the CIA, the SAS, and Mossad*. New York: Pegasus Books, 2010.

———. *Soldiers of Fortune: A History of the Mercenary in Modern Warfare*. New York: Pegasus Books, 2009.

Gillespie, Robert M. *Black Ops Vietnam: The Operational History of MACVSOG*. Annapolis: Naval Institute Press, 2011.

Gormly, Robert A. *Combat Swimmer: Memoirs of a Navy SEAL*. New York: Penguin Onyx, 1999.

Haney, Eric L. *Inside Delta Force: The Story of America's Elite Counterterrorist Unit*. New York: Delacorte Press, 2002.

Harclerode, Peter. *Secret Soldiers: Special Forces in the War against Terrorism*. London: Cassell, 2000.

Hersh, Seymour M. *Chain of Command: The Road from 9/11 to Abu Ghraib*. New York: Harper Perennial, 2005.

Hoe, Alan. *The Quiet Professional: Major Richard J. Meadows of the U.S. Army Special Forces*. Lexington: University Press of Kentucky, 2011.

Holcomb, John B., et al. "Causes of Death in U.S. Special Operations Forces in the Global War on Terrorism: 2001–2004." *Annals of Surgery* 245, no. 6 (2007): 986–91.

Hoyt, Edwin P. *SEALs at War: The Story of U.S. Navy Special Warfare*. New York: Dell Books, 1993.

Isby, David C. *Leave No Man Behind: Liberation and Capture Missions*. London: Weidenfeld & Nicolson, 2004.

Jones, Seth G. *Hunting in the Shadows: The Pursuit of Al Qa'ida since 9/11*. New York: W. W. Norton, 2012.

Kelly, Orr. *From a Dark Sky: The Story of U.S. Air Force Special Operations*. Novato, CA: Presidio Press, 1996.

Kyle, Christopher, with Scott McEwen and Jim DeFelice. *American Sniper: The Autobiography of the Most Lethal Sniper in U.S. Military History*. New York: William Morrow, 2013.

Kyle, James H. *The Guts to Try: The Untold Story of the Iran Hostage Rescue Mission by the On-Scene Desert Commander.* New York: Ballantine Books, 2002.

Leebaert, Derek. *To Dare and to Conquer: Special Operations and the Destiny of Nations, from Achilles to Al Qaeda.* New York: Little, Brown, 2006.

Lutz, Catherine. *Homefront: A Military City and the American Twentieth Century.* Boston: Beacon Press, 2001.

MacCloskey, Monro. *Secret Air Missions: Counterinsurgency Operations in Southern Europe.* New York: Richards Rosen Press, 1966.

Marcinko, Richard, with John Weisman. *Rogue Warrior.* New York: Pocket Books, 1992.

Mazzetti, Mark. *The Way of the Knife: The CIA, a Secret Army, and the War at the Ends of the Earth.* New York: Penguin, 2013.

McChrystal, Stanley. *My Share of the Task: A Memoir.* New York: Portfolio/Penguin, 2013.

McRaven, William H. *Spec Ops: Case Studies in Special Operations Warfare. Theory and Practice.* New York: Ballantine Books, 1995.

Moore, Robin. *Hunting Down Saddam: The Inside Story of the Search and Capture.* New York: St. Martin's, 2004.

———. *Major Mike: Major Mike Williams as told to Robin Moore.* New York: Ace Books, 1980.

———. *The Green Berets.* New York: Crown Books, 1965.

Morris, R. C. *The Ether Zone: U.S. Army Special Forces Detachment B-52, Project Delta.* Ashland, OR: Hellgate Press, 2009.

Owen, Mark, with Kevin Maurer. *No Easy Day: The Firsthand Account of the Mission That Killed Osama bin Laden.* New York: Dutton, 2012.

Paddock, Alfred H., Jr. *U.S. Army Special Warfare: Its Origins.* Washington, DC: National Defense University Press, 1982.

Plaster, John L. *Secret Commandos: Behind Enemy Lines with the Elite Warriors of SOG.* New York: NAL Caliber, 2005.

———. *SOG: A Photo History of the Secret Wars.* Boulder, CO: Paladin Press, 2000.

———. *SOG: The Secret Wars of America's Commandos in Vietnam.* New York: Penguin Onyx, 1998.

Pushies, Fred. *Deadly Blue: Battle Stories of the U.S. Air Force Special Operations Command.* New York: American Management Association, 2009.

Robinson, Tina. *Masters of Chaos: The Secret History of the Special Forces.* New York: Public Affairs Press, 2004.

Rogers, Anthony. *Someone Else's War: Mercenaries from 1960 to the Present.* New York: HarperCollins, 1998.

Royal, Joseph. "Casualty Wounding Patterns in Special Operations Forces in Operation Iraqi Freedom." *Journal of Special Operations Medicine* 8, no. 2 (2008): 55–60.

Sasser, Charles W. *Raider: The True Story of the Legendary Soldier Who Performed More POW Raids Than Any Other American in History.* New York: St. Martin's Press, 2002.

Schroen, Gary C. *First In: An Insider's Account of How the CIA Spearheaded the War on Terror in Afghanistan.* New York: Ballantine Books, 2005.

Shultz, Richard H., Jr. *The Secret War against Hanoi: Kennedy's and Johnson's Use of Spies, Saboteurs and Covert Warriors in North Vietnam.* New York: HarperCollins, 1999.

Simpson, Charles M. *Inside the Green Berets: The First Thirty Years.* Novato, CA: Presidion Press, 1983.

Stanton, Doug. *Horse Soldiers: The Extraordinary Story of a Band of U.S. Soldiers Who Rode to Victory in Afghanistan.* New York: Scribner, 2009.

Stanton, Martin. *Somalia on $5 a Day: A Soldier's Story.* New York: Ballantine Books, 2001.

Stanton, Shelby L. *Green Berets at War: US Army Special Forces in Southeast Asia, 1956–1975.* New York: Dell Books, 1985.

Stein, Jeff. *A Murder in Wartime: The Untold Spy Story That Changed the Course of the Vietnam War.* New York: St. Martin's Press, 1992.

Tourison, Sedgwick. *Project Alpha: Washington's Secret Military Operations in North Vietnam.* New York: St. Martin's, 1997.

Trest, Warren A. *Air Commando One: Heinie Aderholt and America's Secret Wars*. Washington, DC: Smithsonian Institution Press, 2000.

Waller, Douglas C. *The Commandos: The Inside Story of America's Secret Soldiers*. New York: Dell Books, 1995.

Waugh, Billy, with Tim Keown. *Hunting the Jackal: A Special Forces and CIA Soldier's Fifty Years on the Frontline of the War against Terrorism*. New York: Avon Books, 2004.

Weiss, Mitch, and Kevin Maurer. *Hunting Che: How a U.S. Special Forces Team Helped Capture the World's Most Famous Revolutionary*. New York: Berkley Caliber, 2013.

Y'Blood, William T. *Air Commandos against Japan: Allied Special Operations in World War II Burma*. Annapolis: Naval Institute Press, 2008.

Zedric, Lance Q. *Silent Warriors of World War II: The Alamo Scouts behind Japanese Lines*. Ventura, CA: Pathfinder Press, 1995.

INDEX